River Houses Rising

The Rise of Safe Houses of Hope And Prayer

Revised & Updated

By R. Maurice Smith

© Copyright 2011, 2014. Rising River Media.
All rights reserved.

2014 Revised Edition

Written permission must be secured from the publisher to use or reproduce any part of this work in any form except where quotations are accompanied by a full and accurate recitation of the work's full title, the publisher, and the publisher's address. Additional copies of this publication are available from the address given below:

Published by Rising River Media, P. O. Box 9133, Spokane, Washington 99209

www.risingrivermedia.org

Cover design & original art work by Gale A. Smith.
Cover photo and inside art licensed through istock.

Unless otherwise noted, all Scripture quotations are from The Holy Bible, English Standard Version (ESV), Copyright 2001 by Crossway Bibles, a publishing ministry of Good News Publishers. Used by permission. All rights reserved.

ISBN 13   978-0-9960096-2-1

Other Titles Available From Rising River Media

And They Dreamt Of A Kingdom
Biblical Reflections On Discipleship And The Kingdom Of God - Volume 1

All Dogs Go To Heaven, Don't They?
Biblical Reflections On Christian Universalism and Ultimate Reconciliation

Preparing For The Coming Spiritual Outpouring
Reflections On The Coming Move of God's Spirit

Safe Houses of Hope And Prayer
Your Practical Guide To Organic Church In Your House

The Least of These
The Role of Good Deeds In A Jesus-Shaped Spirituality

The Inextinguishable Blaze
God's Call To Holiness, Repentance, Intimacy and Spiritual Awakening

When Jesus Visits His Church
A Study Of The Seven Churches of Asia (Revelation Chapters 2-3)

You Wanna Do What In Your House?!
Straight Answers To Your Most Frequently Asked Questions About House Church

All titles are available on our website at ***www.risingrivermedia.org*** from Amazon.com!

Table of Contents

Table of Contents (5)

Author's Preface (7)

Introduction (9)

The Sound And Smell of Rain (19)

The Bucket That Rube Built (25)

A Church For The Rest of Us (29)

Red Skies And House Churches (35)

A Holy Discontent (47)

The Kingdom In Your House (53)

"River Houses" (63)

Pursuing A Jesus-Shaped Spirituality (73)

It's Time To "Just Do It" (87)

A Time To Dance (101)

Discovering People Of Peace (107)

Contagious DNA (117)

God Has A Math Problem (131)

Rabbits, Elephants And Mules (139)

A Time To Network - Part 1 (153)

A Time To Network - Part 2 (157)

Author's Preface

To The Revised Edition

Every author is painfully aware that there is no perfect book, or even a finished one. Before the printer's ink is even dry on the first copy, something pops up to remind the author that nothing is ever truly finished. Important facts or quoted statistics change, typos emerge, new information comes to light that you wish you had included, or a reader points out an unfinished thought, an incomplete sentence or a missing footnote. The list could go on . . . and on.

In the three years since I wrote the original version of this book I have experienced all of the above (and then some). The list has grown sufficiently long that an updated and revised edition of this book and its companion volume *(Safe Houses of Hope And Prayer: Your Practical Guide to Organic Church In Your House*) is warranted. In particular, this update has provided me with the opportunity to connect concepts expressed in this book with their further expansion and development in subsequent books which had not been written at the time of the original book. What has not changed between the original version and this revised edition is my primary thesis, namely, that in our generation God is raising up a new vessel through which He intends to move in great power and blessing in revival and spiritual awakening. That vessel is organic house church. This book, updated and revised, offers a practical starting point for your own personal journey into what God is doing in our day. Welcome to the journey.

Introduction

"He has made everything beautiful in its time. Also, he has put eternity into man's heart, yet so that he cannot find out what God has done from the beginning to the end." (Ecclesiastes 3:11)

When it comes to issues of faith, discipleship and the Kingdom of God, we all have two basic needs. On the one hand we all need a God-breathed vision that is greater than the sum of us, our efforts and our labors. We need a vision we can "wrap our hearts around" without ever exhausting it or losing our sense of both fear and wonder. I believe this is why God has placed eternity in our hearts. We all experience an "eternal heart ache" that continually challenges our hearts and calls us to explore both the greatness and the "wildness" of this Kingdom He has established and *"which shall have no end"* (Isaiah 9:7; Luke 1:33).

On the other hand each of us has the need for a practical, tangible expression of this eternal ache, this Kingdom, that is small and practical enough for us to wrap our heads around and to say *"I can do this!"* It is often true that our hearts long for more than our heads can fully comprehend. That is the challenge of the Christian life; to comprehend the incomprehensible, to believe the impossible, to pray for the miraculous and to manifest eternity in the limited space of our own lives.

River Houses Rising

It has been said that the Kingdom of God is an ocean that an elephant can swim in, and a pool that a child can wade in. It is both, and yet it is more. And in the plan of God the Church is supposed to be the place where anyone can come and experience an authentic and genuine manifestation of that Kingdom for themselves, where each of us can touch and taste *"the powers of the age to come"* (Hebrews 6:5). Our challenge as believers is to communicate these realities to a culture that has given up on finding anything wondrous or eternal in traditional expressions of Church as they have known it. From their limited perspective, the music, the message and the special effects are better at the movies, or at a Garth Brooks concert.

In any venture like this there will be "nay sayers" who will condemn what they don't understand, and will be quick to accuse us of emblazoning eternity on a bumper sticker, or reducing faith, discipleship and the Kingdom of God to nothing more than a book, a program and a window decal. Personally, I'm willing to take that risk. Why? Because faith stops growing when we stop taking risks. And because the reward is so potentially huge.

Consider Yourself Warned

"One of the reasons I believe our conventional churches aren't multiplying is because God doesn't want to multiply them." - Author Neil Cole - Posted on Twitter.

I want to give you fair warning. If the above quote from my

Introduction

friend, Neil Cole, upsets you, then you should probably stop reading now. It will only get worse! Sorry. But this book is NOT for the faint of heart. It isn't for those who think that everything is fine in "Churchdom," or that any problems that do exist in the Church can be solved with hard work and another program.

This book isn't for the comfortable or the complacent. If you are content to live in the Church of Laodicea[1] where everything is lukewarm and comfortable - the worship is comfortable, the message is comfortable and the flavored espresso in the Café is lukewarm - then let me suggest that you stay where you are. Or if you are a "religionist" who believes that people and the Church function best when engaging in religious activities and living by carefully crafted sets of rules (as well as by unwritten expectations), then this book is not for you. In fact, you should probably stop reading now and run for cover. I think God is about to rudely shake your comfortable religious paradigm that you call "church." And if you aren't ready to listen to any warning I might offer you, it's probably best that you to stay right where you are for now. Neither of us needs to irritate the other unnecessarily. Take the blue pill, Neo, and go back to sleep.

But if you are already experiencing a "holy discontent," a

---

[1] See Revelation 3:14-22. Laodicea was the last of the seven churches of Asia in Revelation Chapters 2-3 addressed by the risen Christ. See our book, **When Jesus Visits His Church: A Study Of The Seven Churches of Asia (Revelation Chapters 2-3)**, available on our website at www.risingrivermedia.org from Amazon.com.

River Houses Rising

spiritual hunger for something more and greater than you have experienced so far in your life, then you may be ready for what this book is all about. But be warned. It means taking the red pill.

Don't Get Boxed In

The principles I am about to share in this book can be implemented anywhere. They are about life in the Kingdom of God, not about conduct appropriate to a building - even a house. As Steven reminded the 1st Century Jewish religious leaders of his day, the Scriptures have always taught that God doesn't live in "boxes" of human construction, whether temples, cathedrals or houses.

"Yet the Most High does not dwell in houses made by hands, as the prophet says, 'Heaven is my throne, and the earth is my footstool. What kind of house will you build for me, says the Lord, or what is the place of my rest?'" (Acts 7:48-49)

Rather than man made boxes, the New Testament clearly teaches us that God has chosen to take up residence in one of the most fragile of all structures - the human heart. We - you and I - are the building where God now dwells through faith in Christ. For this simple yet profound reason, whenever individuals exercise faith, submit their hearts to God's rule and His Kingdom and gather together, they ARE the Church, regardless of where they happen to be. This gathering of "disciples of the Kingdom" can take place anywhere: in a house, a coffee shop, a business office, a homeless men's

Introduction

shelter, a public park, a college dorm, and yes, even in a church building.

But along with this profound truth of *"Christ in you, the hope of glory"* comes an equally profound warning. Beware the always-lurking tendency to re-create new boxes after old ones have been destroyed. This warning is necessary because the most profound religious box of all is not to be found in a building, but in our hearts - right alongside the God Who desires to reign there. Somewhere in the recesses of our hearts there is a part of us that longs to put God back into a box of our creation. Once captured in our box we can turn Him into a tame lion for public display and for our personal entertainment. We can set rules for how He will behave and how we can control Him to our benefit. And the process of creating a religion-shaped spirituality, shaped like a box of our creation, starts all over again. Be warned. He is not a tame lion. And He doesn't like boxes.

Don't Get The Wrong Impression

Some people reading this book might get the wrong impression, that I am some how "anti-Church" or I am "angry" with the institutional Church. That would be a wrong impression. Indeed, I am a child of the institutional Church. I was raised from an early age in the United Methodist Church by loving and sincere parents who believed in the importance of Church involvement. My elderly mother is a licensed lay speaker in the United Methodist Church (and even has a sermon clip on YouTube!). I came to saving faith

River Houses Rising

in a traditional Southern Baptist Church at the tail end of the Jesus Movement. I did street ministry in Fayetteville, North Carolina among GIs returning from Southeast Asia during the waning days of the Vietnam War. I then became a "campus Christian radical" at the university of North Carolina (Chapel Hill) during the 1970s and helped lead a spiritual awakening on that campus. After two years on staff with Campus Crusade for Christ, I left to study Christian theology and apologetics at Denver Seminary under Gordon R. Lewis. I have planted churches, split churches (Oh yes, that was fun) and have served in a variety of official positions ranging from youth director, ruling elder, administrator and pastor. You get the idea. I am a child and product of the traditional institutional Church. I have personally experienced some of the best and the worst that conventional expressions of Church have to offer (and have miraculously survived with my faith intact!).

But at the end of the day, I am a contemporary believer who is absolutely convinced that the Church in the West is quickly losing its battle with materialism, secularism and Postmodernism. I am equally convinced that the only hope for the Church and our culture is a divine visitation of historic, even biblical, proportions which will manifest itself and flow like a river through new channels called organic house churches, what we are calling *Safe Houses of Hope And Prayer.*

You should also understand early on that I did not choose the house church movement. By God's Providential

Introduction

workings, it chose me. Following a disastrous business failure and bankruptcy, my wife and I fell into the house church movement through the back door. Our journey into house church reminds me of British author G. K. Chesterton, who begins his classic book, **Orthodoxy**, with the whimsical notion of *"an English yachtsman who slightly miscalculated his course and discovered England under the impression that it is a new island in the South Seas."*[2] That, said Chesterton, represented his own story of discovering Christian faith in Christianized England. *"What could be more delightful,"* observed Chesterton, *"than to have in the same few minutes all the fascinating terrors of going abroad combined with all the humane security of coming home again."* Chesterton's description of his own journey into Christian faith is also an apt description of the journey of many people into house church, including my own.

Further Up And Further In

The purpose of this book is really quite simple. It is to encourage you to become part of the story now being written about what God is doing in our day. It is that same story of world redemption and the arrival of the Kingdom of God that was proclaimed two thousand years ago by Jesus of Nazareth. God is now calling out and raising up disciples of His Kingdom who will manifest His Kingdom presence to a new generation through new vessels of organic house

---

[2]G. K. Chesterton, **Orthodoxy** (New York: Image/Doubleday, 2001), p. 2.

River Houses Rising

churches, meeting in a wide variety of organic places including homes just like yours. We are calling these organic house churches *Safe Houses of Hope And Prayer* and we believe God wants to start one in your house. Are you willing to partner with Him?

A final warning is needed here. Beware the adventure you are about to embark upon. Life outside of the comfortable religious (or non-religious) box you have been accustomed to can be both challenging and exciting. There is a "wonder and wildness" to life in the Kingdom of God - a divine unpredictability - that the box-bound religionist (or secularist) cannot appreciate or understand. This is what those twelve fishermen, peasants and social outcasts Jesus first called to be His disciples quickly discovered for themselves. The "wonder and wildness" of the Kingdom of God challenged those twelve men to their very core, even causing one of them to fall by the way side as a spiritual casualty of the encounter. But for those who continued on, they discovered a spiritual adventure they never could have imagined during their days of being box-bound religionists.

In his final installment of **The Chronicles of Narnia**, entitled **The Last Battle**, C.S. Lewis summed up the sense of fulfillment that all spiritual adventurers sense when they realize that they have found what they had always looked for. It is the sense of joy and fulfillment experienced when believers set out in search of "church" and instead discover "a Kingdom." At that moment they echo the words of Bree the Unicorn who declared: *"I have come home at last! This is my*

Introduction

real country! I belong here. This is the land I have been looking for all my life, though I never knew it till now. The reason why we loved the old Narnia is because it sometimes looked a little like this. Bree-hee-hee! Come further up, come further in." [3]

This is the call of God to believers, spiritual pilgrims, sojourners and disciples even today as He beckons us into the Kingdom of God and into the new manifestation of that Kingdom known as organic house church, a manifestation we are calling *Safe Houses of Hope And Prayer*.

This is your invitation to *"Come further up! Come further in!"*

---

[3] C. S. Lewis, ***The Last Battle***, in ***The Complete Chronicles of Narnia*** (New York: Harper Collins, 1998), page 520.

River Houses Rising

Chapter 1

The Sound And Smell of Rain

"And Elijah said to Ahab, 'Go up, eat and drink, for there is a sound of the rushing of rain.'" (1 Kings 18:41)

It happened on a Wednesday evening. Our house church had gathered in a home in the Spokane Valley. Ten of us were gathered in the family room just off of the covered (but open) deck with the door leading to the deck open for fresh air. A promise of rain hung in the air as clouds had moved into the area that afternoon. About mid-way into our gathering, as we prayed and worshiped together, we all became aware of the sound of falling rain, and the breeze through the open door filled the room with the sweet smell of rain. It was a strong rain, too. You just knew if you went outside you would quickly be soaked. We even joked that we hoped everyone had rolled the windows up in their cars. One person commented that he wished he had brought his coat. Others commented that they just loved the smell of fresh falling rain.

After celebrating communion and concluding our time together, people began to leave. A few minutes later two people returned with a stunning announcement. There had been NO rain. The cars, the grass, the streets, everything, was bone dry. Not a drop of rain. People went out into the back yard to see if it was one of those freak rains that falls in

River Houses Rising

the back yard but not across the street. But everything was bone dry (and, no, they didn't even have a sprinkler system that could be mistaken for rain!).

We were stunned - dumbfounded! We had ALL heard, smelled and commented on the rain (a digital recorder which ran during the meeting even recorded the sound of the rain along with our comments about it)! But there was no rain! Finally, I suggested to the group what was quickly becoming obvious to us all. God was at work in our midst. God had allowed us to hear what Elijah heard - the sound of a yet-future rain storm. He had given us a "prophetic sign" regarding what He is about to do in the midst of His Church. Rain is coming. A Spiritual Outpouring of unprecedented, incredible power is on its way. And He wants you to know about it . . . and to be a part of it. God wants it to rain in your house.

Life By The Bucket

I have lived, worked and spent time in parts of the world where people depend on rainfall as one of their chief sources of water. In those places life and architecture are structured to take advantage of every passing storm. Elaborate systems of gutters on buildings lead to collection vessels, and every house has an in-ground cistern where water is collected and stored. Simply put, life depends upon buckets to catch the life-sustaining rain.

There is a practical lesson here for you and me. You and I

The Sound And Smell of Rain

can't control the weather or the timing of rain storms. But there is something we can do while we await the coming rain. We can prepare our buckets. As people whose very lives depend upon the rain already know, during the dry season you prepare your vessels, so that when the rainy season arrives you are ready to collect every life-giving drop.

Rain is coming. Are you ready for what God is about to do in our day? Is your bucket ready?

What God Is Doing In Our Day

"If you would make the greatest success of your life, try to discover what God is doing in your time, and fling yourself into the accomplishment of His purpose and will." - Arthur Wallis

This quote from Arthur Wallis is really quite profound. Take just a moment and reflect on it. Now, I want to ask you four simple questions:

1. Do you want your life to be as successful as possible?
2. Do you know what God is doing in our day?
3. Do you want to know?
4. Do you want to be a part of it?

O.K., if you have an IQ above that of a turnip the answer to the first question should be obvious. Of course we want our lives to be as successful as possible! The real challenge here becomes how we define "success" in our materialistic age

River Houses Rising

that measures success by budgets, bank accounts, buildings and "bling"!

From this point on the questions get more challenging. Consider the second one: *Do you know what God is doing in our day?* Could you sum it up in a paragraph that you could explain to your spouse or to a neighbor? Most people don't know, and that includes most professing Christians. Most Christians live quiet lives of "blissful ignorance" going through religious activities (including the Church-sponsored mission trip to build a house for a family in a third world country), never understanding what God is doing in the world around them, and never knowing what their part of God's plan could have been. Ouch!

Christian author A.W. Tozer is reputed to have said, *"If you want to be happy, don't pray for discernment."*[4] Wise words from a man who spent his career and Christian life praying for discernment. And that leads to the third question: *Do you want to know what God is doing?* Be careful how you answer this question. Why? Well, for two reasons. *First,* if you truly want to know, then chances are very good that God will show you. And, *second*, if God shows you what He is doing in our world today you will be confronted with a choice: do you obey, or do you stay (where you are)? Like the character Neo in the blockbuster movie *"The Matrix,"* do you take "the blue

---

[4] A. W. Tozer, ***The Purpose of Man: Designed To Worship,*** Compiled and Edited by James L. Snyder (Ventura, CA: Regal, 2009), p. 14.

The Sound And Smell of Rain

pill" and wake up in your comfortable bed, or do you take "the red pill" and discover an adventure beyond your imagination.

And this leads us to the final and fateful question: *Do you want to be a part of what God is doing in our day?* I believe that we are standing today on the eve of the greatest spiritual awakening and outpouring the Western Church has experienced in well over 100 years.[5] Rain is coming and it is time to get our buckets in order. This coming rain will become a River of God's Spirit which will flow in spiritual power and blessing unknown in the experience of our generation. God is preparing His end-time harvest. And to accommodate that harvest He is raising up tens of thousands of organic, multiplying house churches led by believers just like you. These organic house churches, meeting in homes like yours and led by Kingdom-minded disciples like you, will be the new "buckets" - the vessels - for what God is doing in our day. And He is calling you to be a part of it. The only question remaining is this: *Are you ready to become a part of what God is doing in our day?*

Safe Houses of Hope And Prayer is the name we have given to this new network of organic house church "buckets," God's new vessels to catch and keep the rain of this coming

---

[5] We have written extensively about this coming move of God's Spirit. First, see ***The Inextinguishable Blaze: God's Call To Holiness, Repentance, Intimacy And Spiritual Awakening***, and ***Preparing For The Coming Spiritual Outpouring: Reflections On the Coming Move of God's Spirit.*** Both books are available on our website from Amazon.com.

River Houses Rising

Spiritual Outpouring. And He wants YOUR house to be one of them!

Chapter 2

The Bucket That Rube Built

Buckets are very simple vessels. Or at least they're supposed to be simple. It's hard to complicate a bucket. Unless, of course, you're either a professional church planter, or you're Rube Goldberg. And therein lies an organic house church equipping parable.

Rube Goldberg, Church Planter

I'm convinced that "Rube" Goldberg must have been a church planter. I say that because there are SO MANY people who honestly believe that something as simple as being the Church must be done in the most complicated way possible.

Reuben Lucius Goldberg (1883-1970) was born in San Francisco, studied engineering at UC Berkeley and went to work as an engineer with the City of San Francisco Water and Sewers Department. But his heart was elsewhere. He loved to illustrate cartoons, a talent which eventually led him to New York where he built a career drawing daily cartoons for the *Evening Mail*. "Rube" Goldberg became known for his "INVENTIONS," cartoons which illustrated and symbolized man's willingness to exert the maximum effort possible in order to accomplish minimal results. There were essentially two ways to do things, he believed. There was the easy way

River Houses Rising

and the hard way. And his illustrations lampooned the reality that a surprising number of people preferred doing things the hard way.

It was at this point in my research that I came to the painful realization that Rube Goldberg must have had a secret career teaching church growth workshops. After all, I mused, how else could we explain a philosophy of ministry and church that results in simple tasks like following Jesus and being His Church becoming so complex? What other explanation could there be to the reality that it now requires multi-million dollar facilities, professional musicians and highly educated guys with theology and business degrees to manage what Jesus of Nazareth entrusted to twelve uneducated fishermen and social outcasts? Those uneducated fishermen and social outcasts turned the Roman Empire upside down. Two thousand years later, our highly educated professional staff is still working on reaching New Jersey.

Question: How many church staffers does it take to change a light bulb?

Answer: We aren't sure. The Sunday school teacher mentioned it to the elder for Adult Education who submitted a request for light bulbs to the elder board which then passed the request on to the elder for building and grounds. But he argued that it was really a matter for the volunteer janitorial team, none of whom could be reached. So a motion to table action on light bulbs was made, seconded and passed. In the

The Bucket That Rube Built

mean time, an enterprising staffer found several spare light bulbs in the janitor's closet and proceeded to replace the bad bulbs himself. The elders are now debating disciplinary proceedings against the staffer for failure to submit to proper authority. The disciplinary action, along with the still pending request for light bulbs, will be taken up at the next regularly scheduled board meeting.

And that strange whirring noise you may be hearing is an INVENTION, one which is helping Rube Goldberg to spin in his grave (actually, it's rotating the coffin counter-clockwise on its longitudinal axis while at the same time spinning it end-over-end. Rube would be pleased).

Questions For Reflection

Reflect on an example from your own experience where a person or organization insisted on doing things "the hard way" (or the more complicated way) when a simple alternative was available?

If Jesus could entrust His church to simple fishermen, tax collectors and other social outcasts, what prevents Him from entrusting that same church to you and me today?

Safe Houses of Hope And Prayer represents a return to the simplicity of being the Church as envisioned by Jesus and practiced by the early Church. It is simple, organic church in your house! Are you ready?

River Houses Rising

Chapter 3

A Church For The Rest of Us

Trust me when I say that the *"let's do it the hard way"* spirit Rube Goldberg lampooned is still alive, well and planting churches today! I recently visited the website of a prominent "church planting network" where I read an article on the 20 (count them, 20) characteristics of anyone desiring to become a church planter. The implication was clear: if you couldn't demonstrate these 20 characteristics you really shouldn't even think about trying to plant a church. It was an impressive list. So impressive, in fact, that I doubt the twelve fishermen and social misfits that Jesus chose as His disciples could have qualified. In fact, based on those 20 "qualifications" I think they probably would have put Jesus on probation to see if He could measure up. After all, we need to sort out the riff raff.

Maybe you remember the story from the Civil War. In late 1861 President Abraham Lincoln placed General George B. McClellan in charge of the Union Army of the Potomac. General McClellan was a competent professional soldier who took the rag-tag and demoralized Union Army and instilled a sense of pride, military discipline and professionalism. His only problem was a stubborn reluctance to use his newly trained troops in battle. McClellan's refusal to fight exasperated President Lincoln who finally declared to a group of top Generals, *"If General McClellan does not want*

River Houses Rising

to use the army, I would like to borrow it for a time." [6]

Funny stuff, until we realize that it also expresses how Jesus feels about His Church. Jesus wants His Church back. But He isn't interested in just "borrowing" it from the Generals for a while. He wants to take it back from the professionals who have misused it for things other than His Kingdom purposes, and He wants to return it to people who will love Him, follow Him and obey Him in His mission to proclaim the good news of the Kingdom of God. He wants to take His Church back from the "professionals" and give it to "the others."

A Church For The "Others"

"After this the Lord appointed seventy-two others and sent them on ahead of him, two by two, into every town and place where he himself was about to go. And he said to them, 'The harvest is plentiful, but the laborers are few. Therefore pray earnestly to the Lord of the harvest to send out laborers into his harvest.'"

We know the names of Jesus' twelve disciples. You can read them for yourself in Matthew Chapter 10. But do you know the names of the seventy-two "others" in this passage? In this particular chapter Jesus is sending out seventy-two people as "harvest workers" - Church planters, if you will -

---

[6] This comment took place on January 10, 1862 during a war planning session with Lincoln's top Generals. See James M. McPherson, **Tried by War: Abraham Lincoln as Commander in Chief** (New York: Penguin Press HC, 2008) p. 66.

A Church For The Rest of Us

and we know absolutely nothing about them! There is no mention of their "qualifications" for such an important task, except that they were willing to do what Jesus told them to do. And that's the point. They had no "qualifications" to speak of, but Jesus was willing to entrust them with leadership in His Kingdom and in His Church. [7] And in our present age of ministry professionals, that alone is an eye-popping contrast.

The early Church that Jesus founded was a Church filled with and led by "others." They were fishermen, carpenters, political activists (called Zealots), former tax collectors, slaves and more. They were ordinary people who heard the call of the Kingdom of God, responded in faith and followed Jesus. They were "the others," ordinary people whose faith and obedience changed the world.

A Church That Fred Could Lead

I suspect that "the others" who made up the early New Testament Church were not unlike my friend Fred. I met Fred through an outreach in the West Central neighborhood of Spokane. Fred grew up in the Aryan Nations. He went to prison at an early age, became involved with drugs, became a "soldier" (enforcer) in the California drug world working for various drug gangs. He became a dealer, a user and an enforcer. On one particular Monday evening as I was

---

[7] In our book, ***And They Dreamt Of A Kingdom***, we discuss how non-noteworthy Jesus' twelve disciples were before Jesus called them to "Follow me." See *"Lesson 25 - And Then There Were Twelve"* in that book for our discussion of the twelve.

River Houses Rising

barbecuing hot dogs for a couple hundred people at the neighborhood outreach I heard a commotion. Someone came to me saying that Fred had just shot his finger off. I dropped what I was doing, went across the street and found Fred, sitting on a stool, surrounded by people and bleeding profusely from his hand. Sure enough, he had shot the third digit of his little finger off while cleaning an illegal gun which had been rigged to misfire and kill him in a drug-deal-gone-bad. I prayed for him while we waited for the paramedics and police to arrive and take Fred away.

Soon after that evening Fred became involved in our outreach and his life began to change. When he was sent to prison on an old drug trafficking charge I testified on his behalf at his sentencing (five months in prison). When the time came for him to surrender himself at the local jail we held a "going to jail party" in his apartment. I corresponded with him in prison, arranged for another old warrant to be quashed so he could be released on time and picked him up in Seattle when the Department of Corrections released him by dropping him off at the public library there.

While in prison Fred had gotten clean from drugs, made a renewed profession of faith in Christ and decided that he wanted to pursue a new life. I had the privilege of performing the wedding for Fred and his wife, Julia, and later baptized Fred into his new-found faith.

Drugs and a hard life have left both Fred and Julie on a small disability income, but they still want to follow Jesus in a life of

A Church For The Rest of Us

obedience. Fred wants to be a "street shepherd" in his neighborhood, steering others away from the life he once embraced. And Jesus wants a Church that "the others" like Fred can attend, even lead, without trumped up qualifications or religious condemnation.

And Fred is not alone. There are countless "others" whom Jesus wants to fill and lead His Church. They are people like Alan who builds houses in Hawaii and leads a house church of twenty people in his home on Sunday mornings. They are people like Doug in Spokane who has worked as a postal mail carrier for twenty years and is an avid hunter in his spare time. He and his wife have attended a growing local megachurch for many years. But Jesus is now calling Doug and his wife to start a house church in their home and to prepare for the coming Spiritual Outpouring. They are people like Garold and Kitty who lead a house church in their home on Wednesday evenings and have seen numerous people healed and delivered from demonic oppression in their living room. What are their qualifications? Kitty is a homemaker and Garold repairs welders for a living and rebuilds classic cars in his spare time. But God has called and gifted both of them to lead His new Church made up of "others" just like themselves.

These are just a few of the countless "others": bus drivers, mattress salesmen, school teachers, college students, street people and more. People God is calling out and raising up to fill and lead His Church. How about you? Are you one of "the others" whom Jesus is calling and sending? Are you ready?

River Houses Rising

I hope so, because there is an urgency to all of this that you need to understand.

Questions For Reflection

Why are the qualifications of the ordinary, unnamed seventy-two "others" any different from your qualifications?

Safe Houses of Hope And Prayer represent organic church for the rest of us. It is all about Jesus taking back His Church, taking it away from the professionals and giving it back to "the others" He originally intended it for. People like Fred, Alan, Doug, Garold and YOU. It is simple organic Church in your house!

Chapter 4

Red Skies And House Churches

"And the Pharisees and Sadducees came, and to test him they asked him to show them a sign from heaven. He answered them, 'When it is evening, you say, 'It will be fair weather, for the sky is red.' And in the morning, 'It will be stormy today, for the sky is red and threatening.' You know how to interpret the appearance of the sky, but you cannot interpret the signs of the times.'" (Matthew 16:1-3)

As we noted at the close of the previous chapter, there is an urgency to what God is doing in our day, and that urgency brings us to the topic of "the weather."

Understanding The Weather

Only a fool ignores the weather. That was Jesus' point. The ancient mariners had a saying that went something like this:

> *"Red sky at night, a sailor's delight;*
> *Red sky at morning, sailor take warning."*

Everyone in Jesus' day understood that only a fool would venture out onto the water in the face of obvious warnings regarding approaching bad weather. It wasn't just a matter of common sense. It was a matter of life and death. Within the context of Matthew 16 the meaning went even deeper:

River Houses Rising

people tend to ignore the obvious signs of God's workings while demanding new signs. Jesus' response was simple but profound. Because they had ignored the obvious signs around them (healing the sick, raising the dead, casting out demons - all messianic signs of the Kingdom of God) they neither needed nor deserved any additional sign (other than the resurrection itself, which he alludes to in 16:4). Spiritually blind people don't need new truths to stare at.

Storm Clouds Over The Church

As we observed at the outset of this Chapter, only a fool ignores the weather, either the physical weather which warns us of pending storms, or the spiritual weather which warns of us of coming spiritual storms. And the spiritual weather of our day is warning us that a storm of biblical proportions is coming. These storm clouds have been gathering over the Church in Europe and America for a number of years, but they have largely been ignored. The problem with storm clouds is that you can only ignore them for so long before they catch up with you and change your world. Here are just a few of those storm clouds over the Church.

Declining Identification. According to the 2008 *Adult Religious Identification Survey* of 54,461 adults, the number of American adults identifying themselves as Christians fell from 86% of American adults in 1990 and to 76% of adults in

Red Skies And House Churches

2008.[8] That's a huge and disturbing decline. According to the authors of the Survey, *"The challenge to Christianity in the U.S. does not come from other religions but rather from a rejection of all forms of organized religion."* They go on to say that the U. S. population continues to show signs of becoming less religious, with one out of every five Americans identifying themselves as *"No stated religious preference."* That category nearly doubled from 8.2% in 1990 to 15.0% in 2008.

Declining Attendance. Sociologist Stanley Presser of the University of Maryland and research assistant Linda Stinson of the U.S. Bureau of Labor Statistics conducted a study in the mid-1990s which found that many Americans were not at church when they claimed to be.[9] Their best estimates found that the percentage of adults who actually attended religious services during the previous weekend dropped from 42% of adults in 1965 to 26% in 1994. Again, a huge decline. This decline was confirmed in 1998 when researchers Hadaway and Marler completed a study of Church attendance and concluded that only 20% of Protestants actually attend Church on Sundays. The results of this study were so disturbing and controversial that Hadaway and Marler

---

[8] ***American Religious Identification Survey (ARIS) 2008***, by Barry A. Kosmin and Ariela Keysar, available on-line at http://commons.trincoll.edu/aris/files/2011/08/ARIS_Report_2008.pdf

[9] *"Data collection mode and social desirability bias in self-reported religious Attendance,"* Stanley Presser; Linda Stinson ***American Sociological Review***; Feb 1998; 63, 1;pg. 137. Available at http://www.stat.columbia.edu/~gelman/stuff_for_blog/church6.pdf

River Houses Rising

repeated the study with a different test group only to receive the same results.[10]

According to a study conducted by LifeWay Christian Resources, the Southern Baptist denomination (the largest Protestant denomination in America) reported a decline in church membership for 2012 of more than 100,000, down 0.7 percent to 15.9 million members and a decline in primary worship attendance of 3.1 percent to 5.97 million. According to LifeWay, baptisms among Southern Baptist Churches in 2012 declined by 5.5 percent to 314,956 people. Reported baptisms among Southern Baptists declined six of the last eight years with 2012 recording the lowest since 1948.

Declining Impact. The standard metrics for measuring the health of "the church" (which all consist of measuring the size and growth of the traditional institutional church) all point toward a church in serious decline, including its impact upon those around us. Simply put, the ground is shaking beneath the American Church. America is becoming less Christian, and fewer professing Christians are attending organized Church. More churches close each year in America than are started. And the number of pastors leaving the ministry (currently estimated at nearly 5,000 per month) is greater

---

[10] See C. Kirk Hadaway and P.L. Marler, *"Did You Really Go To Church This Week?: Behind the Poll Data"* posted on-line at http://www.religion-online.org/showarticle.asp?title=237. See also Tom W. Smith & Seokho Kim, *"The Vanishing Protestant Majority,"* July 2004, NORC/University of Chicago, GSS Social Change Report No. 49, available on-line, www.norc.uchicago.edu/issues/PROTSGO8.pdf.

Red Skies And House Churches

than the number of yearly graduates from all evangelical seminaries in America combined.

Author Reggie McNeal of the Southern Baptist Association documents the collapse of the American Church, *"It's more than numbers."* says McNeal.

"The American culture no longer props up the church the way it did, no longer automatically accepts the church as a player at the table in public life, and can be downright hostile to the church's presence. The collapse I am detailing also involves the realization that values of classic Christianity no longer dominate the way Americans believe or behave." [11]

McNeal goes on to summarize the current situation in the American Church as follows:

"A growing number of people are leaving the institutional church for a new reason. They are not leaving because they have lost faith. They are leaving the church to preserve their faith. They contend that the church no longer contributes to their spiritual development. In fact, they say, quite the opposite. The number of "post-generational" Christians is growing. David Barrett, author of the World Christian Encyclopedia, estimates that there are about 112 million "churchless Christians" world wide, and about 5 percent of all adherents, but he projects that number will double in the next

---

[11] Reggie McNeal, ***The Present Future: Six Tough Questions for the Church*** (San Francisco: John Wiley & Sons, 2003), p. 5

River Houses Rising

twenty five years!" [12]

Storm Clouds of Judgment and Blessing.

There is a quote by Thomas Jefferson inscribed on the wall of the Jefferson Memorial in Washington, D.C. which reads in part, *"Indeed I tremble for my country when I reflect that God is just, that his justice cannot sleep forever."* It is a terrible day in the life of any nation when the justice of God "awakens" and begins to reckon people and nations accountable for their sins. I believe we are entering such a day.

I would dare say that most Christians regard judgment and blessing as irreconcilable opposites - an "either/or" situation. It has to be one or the other, or so they think. But what if God were to do both at once? What if God were to judge the world system, and that part of the Church that has bought in to that system, while sending a spiritual awakening through a new vessel that He is raising up? It would be one of the most challenging times the Church has seen in 500 years.

I have believed and taught for several years that the Church in America stands today between the book of Jeremiah on the one hand, and the book of Acts on the other hand. The great theme of Jeremiah is God's pending judgment upon His people's unrepentant "spiritual adultery," whereas the great theme of the Book of Acts is the Pentecostal outpouring of

---

[12] McNeal, ***The Present Future***, p. 4.

Red Skies And House Churches

the River of God's Spirit to empower the Church. Judgment versus spiritual outpouring; the two opposing yet complimentary sides of God's coming visitation.

Storm Clouds of The End of This Age.

The tension between the two unfolding trends of God's judgment on the one hand and His spiritual outpouring on the other in the years ahead will find expression in spiritual and cultural upheaval of historic (even Biblical) proportions. Consider for just a moment the spiritual, political and economic upheavals which have taken place just since the events of September 11, 2001, or since the economic crisis of 2008. For example, Jerry Twombly is an executive with *"Building God's Way"* and has spent much of his professional career helping Churches and Christian Schools raise money to build and expand. He recently confided in me that he has upset a lot of people by declaring that the age of the megachurch is over. According to Jerry, it is a model of "Church" that is no longer viable in the new economic reality of today.

That is just one of the epic changes currently underway. Political upheaval. Economic upheaval. Moral collapse. Wars in the Middle East. Genocide of Christians by Muslims in Sudan and Darfur. A resurgent and militant Islam. The public persecution of politically incorrect conscience. And what if such upheavals are only the *"beginnings of birth pangs,"* the kinds of epic upheaval that Jesus said would characterize the period just before his return at the end of the age (see

River Houses Rising

Matthew 24)? And if we are indeed approaching the end of the age and Jesus' soon return, then we know at least two things with a high degree of certainty, things which will affect each of us. **First**, we know that things will get progressively worse (occasionally better, but progressively worse). And, **second**, we know that church-as-we-have-known-it will have to change . . . dramatically!

Times of great spiritual revival and awakening often precede or coincide with times of great cultural upheaval and even judgment. It is like standing at the turbulent confluence of two great rivers. On the one hand, the River of God's Spirit, the River of Ezekiel 47, will flow in great power and blessing for spiritual renewal and revival the likes of which have not been seen or experienced in the West in well over 100 years or more. On the other hand, the River of God's judgment upon our increasingly "spiritually adulterous" culture is also preparing to flow in great power.

This is "red sky" weather and it comes with a warning. This is the challenge and the urgency now facing the Church. If God is indeed raising up His end-time Church, then it will be the Church which witnesses those catastrophic events which will precede Jesus' soon return. And it means that there is an urgency to our obedience. It means that time is indeed short and things are going to get much worse, and that requires a new kind of end-time Church.

Red Skies And House Churches

An End-Time Organic Church

If we genuinely believe that we are the Church-at-the-end-of-the-age then we need to come to terms with what that means. It means that church as we have known it will not be able to continue much longer. Economic upheaval may make expensive megachurch buildings and campuses unrealistic, if not impossible. Christians with biblical convictions may find themselves actively persecuted rather than passively tolerated. Churches may lose their tax-exempt status for refusing to accept politically correct agendas regarding gay marriage, hiring practices, and more.[13] These are just a few of the reasons why traditional institutional church as we have known it will not be able to continue much longer.

The signs are all around us that we are running out of time. Jesus is returning soon, and God is calling out and raising up an organic end-time church for His great end-time harvest. But exactly what does it mean to be God's end-time church? We believe it means the following:

---

[13]For example, in *Bob Jones University v. United States, 461 U.S. 574 (1983)*, the United States Supreme Court held that the religion clauses of the First Amendment did not prohibit the Internal Revenue Service from revoking the tax exempt status of a religious university whose practices are contrary to a compelling government public policy, such as eradicating racial discrimination. Could the same legal principle be applied to churches which refuse to hire, ordain or marry practicing homosexuals? See John D. Inazu, *"Religious Freedom vs. LGBT Rights? It's More Complicated,"* JULY 16, 2014, **Christianity Today** online at www.christianitytoday.com.

River Houses Rising

1. A New Organic Vessel. God's end-time organic house churches will be the new vessel - the new wineskin, if you will - for God's great end-time harvest of souls before Jesus returns, led by ordinary people ("the others") just like you. God wants to fill your house with new believers in need of discipleship and encouragement. Isn't that reason enough to be involved?!

2. Small Is The New Big. God's end-time organic house churches will become "big" by staying small; house churches of 15-to-20 people. Like the mustard seed which no one would expect to become great (Matthew 13:31), God's plan is to raise up tens-of-thousands of multiplying house churches in homes like yours. He wants to replace slowly reproducing elephants (traditional "legacy" churches) with rapidly reproducing rabbits (house churches), led by spiritually gifted individuals like you! We'll talk more about this in Chapter 14.

3. A New Spiritual DNA. In addition to becoming small in order to become big, God's end-time organic house churches will be known by three Spirit-breathed qualities, what we refer to as the spiritual DNA of this coming move of God: 1) A Spirit of Holiness and the fear of God (see Isaiah 6:1-8); 2) A Spirit of genuine personal repentance; and 3) A Spirit of genuine personal and corporate intimacy with God. We will talk about these three Spirit-breathed qualities in greater

Red Skies And House Churches

detail in Chapter 12.[14]

4. *Good Deeds.* God's end-time organic house churches will become famous for their commitment to "good deeds," meeting the needs of those around them and for ministry to "the least of these."[15]

Because you are taking the time to read this book, I assume that you are no fool, but are someone who wants to understand and participate in whatever God is doing in our day. And that makes you a rare exception, like the sons of Issachar.

Leaders Versus Followers

"And of the sons of Issachar, men who understood the times, with knowledge of what Israel should do, their chiefs were two hundred; and all their kinsmen were at their command." (1 Chronicles 12:32)

According to the last enumeration of families found in Numbers 26:25 the tribe of Issachar consisted of 64,300 "families" (probably heads of households over age 21). It's

---

[14] We explain these three qualities in detail in our book, ***The Inextinguishable Blaze: God's Call To Holiness, Repentance, Intimacy and Spiritual Awakening***, available on our website from Amazon.com.

[15] See our book, ***The Least of These: The Role of Good Deeds In A Jesus-Shaped Spirituality***, available on our website from Amazon.com.

River Houses Rising

easy to count heads. There are always plenty of them to count. But when it came to numbering those from among the heads who actually understood the times and knew what Israel should do, the number quickly shrank, from 64,300 down to 200.

Followers are relatively easy to find. But finding leaders who can see and understand the "weather" of their time, who can hear from God and who know what He is doing in their day is much more difficult. Just ask the famous sons of Issachar. The ratio there was 1 leader among every 321 followers. Which are you?

This is your call and challenge to leadership in your day. God is looking for and calling out leaders who understand "the weather," the urgency of our time, and who want to be a part of the new thing He is doing in this coming season of spiritual outpouring. Are you one of them?

Questions For Reflection

Take a moment to reflect on the events you see in the world today which give you a sense of urgency in your own spiritual life.

Safe Houses of Hope And Prayer represent a practical response to the urgency of the time in which we live and to the call of God to become the organic house church which meets in your house.

Chapter 5

A Holy Discontent

In the previous Chapter we talked about the urgency of what God is doing in our day. And understanding the urgency of the times in which we live is important. But for some of you reading this book - perhaps even many of you - what you are really wrestling with isn't so much an urgency as it is a deep-seated spiritual discontent, what I call a "holy discontent." And this holy discontent usually takes two forms: spiritual heart burn or spiritual frustration. So, we need to talk about both.

The Children of the Burning Heart

"The moment the Spirit has quickened us to life in regeneration our whole being senses its kinship to God and leaps up in joyous recognition. That is the heavenly birth without which we cannot see the Kingdom of God. It is, however, not an end but an inception, for now begins the glorious pursuit, the heart's happy exploration of the infinite riches of the Godhead. That is where we begin, I say, but where we stop no man has yet discovered, for there is in the awful and mysterious depths of the Triune God neither limit nor end . . . . To have found God and still pursue Him is the soul's paradox of love, scorned indeed by the too-easily-satisfied religionist, but justified in happy

River Houses Rising

*experience by **the children of the burning heart** . . ."* [16]

If this quote from one of my favorite authors, A. W. Tozer, resonates with you, then your "holy discontent" is probably "spiritual heart burn." You are one of *"the children of the burning heart"* whose longing for more of God is not being satisfied through the expressions of traditional church you have experienced thus far. I understand. Children of the burning heart find themselves on a life-long pursuit of God that cannot be satisfied by the spiritual food of a "quick burger, fries and a soda" offered up by the seeker-friendly churches of our day. Indeed they long for a spiritual meal that is nothing less than what Isaiah envisioned, *"On this mountain the LORD of hosts will make for all peoples a feast of rich food, a feast of well-aged wine, of rich food full of marrow, of aged wine well refined."* (Isaiah 25:6)

In both private conversations and public writings I have often described house church as the pursuit of God in the company of friends, and so it is. At the end of the day, house church isn't about evangelism or any other "religious activity." For those who are experiencing this first kind of "holy discontent," organic house church offers the opportunity for the pursuit of God in the company of other *"children of the burning heart"* whose greatest desire is intimacy and fellowship with God and with one another. It is the fellowship of other *"disciples of the Kingdom."*

---

[16] A.W. Tozer, **The Pursuit of God** (Harrisburg, PA: Christian Publications, Inc., 1948), p. 15.

A Holy Discontent

Frustration: Is This All There Is?

The second form of "holy discontent" we need to discuss is a frustration with the current state of things in church-as-we-know-it that is best expressed by the question, *"Is this all there is?"* If you find yourself in this group of people you've probably told yourself something like this: *"I can't help but believe that there's more to loving God and to "church" than what I've experienced so far. Why do I feel this way and what can I do about it?"* Hang onto that thought, because you aren't alone.

At the end of the day, when you turn out the light and go to bed you are frustrated, even disappointed, that church as you've experienced it so far hasn't measured up to what you imagine spirituality and church could be, especially after reading the New Testament. And as you drift off to sleep you hear yourself asking, *"Whatever happened to supernatural, life-changing church like I see in the New Testament?"*

Well, I've got good news for you. You're not alone! Millions of believers around the world are expressing similar feelings and they are starting to do something about it. You and they are part of a huge revolution made up of people who are experiencing the same "holy discontent." They are leaving traditional expressions of church, not because they have lost their faith, but in order to preserve their faith! And many of these spiritual revolutionaries are becoming part of what we are calling the simple church or organic house church movement.

River Houses Rising

House Church in America "By The Numbers"

According to Christian trend watcher and researcher, George Barna, the size of this revolution in America ranges from between 5 million and 20 million people each week (another measure places it at roughly 9-11% of the adult population). According to Barna, the figure of 5 million represents a very conservative definition of those involved in the simple house church movement who see themselves as a complete Church on their own. In other words, instead of "going to church" they have chosen to "become the church." Here are some of the relevant numbers: [17]

22% to 24% of all adults claim to have attended a religious service – not a "worship service" – in someone's home or even in some other place that is independent of a congregational-form church. This would be the "broadest" possible definition of "house church."

10% of the adult population has *"attended a worship service in someone's home, known as a house church"* in the past month.

3% to 6% of all adults say they have been involved in a group of believers that meets regularly in a home or place other than a church building and are not part of a typical

---

[17] The following statistics are based primarily upon surveys conducted by The Barna Group and are available online at https://www.barna.org/barna-update/organic-church. See also George Barna, ***Revolution*** (Wheaton: Tyndale House Publishers, 2005)

A Holy Discontent

church. They are independent, self-governing and consider themselves a complete church on their own.

The Barna Group estimates that more than 70 million adults have at least experimented with some form of house church. In a typical week roughly 20 million adults attend a house church gathering. Over the course of a typical month, that number doubles to about 43 million adults.

Bringing It Together

"Now there were in the church at Antioch prophets and teachers, Barnabas, Simeon who was called Niger, Lucius of Cyrene, Manaen a lifelong friend of Herod the tetrarch, and Saul. While they were worshiping the Lord and fasting, the Holy Spirit said, 'Set apart for me Barnabas and Saul for the work to which I have called them.'" (Acts 13:1-2)

Organic house church has the potential to satisfy the "holy discontent" of our time. It offers the opportunity for the spiritual intimacy so longed for by the *"children of the burning heart"* as well as the supernatural, life-changing church desired by those who are frustrated with traditional church as they have known it.

I believe we can see these spiritual desires coming together in the life of that early house church in Antioch which we read about in Acts 13:1-2. **First**, we see the spiritual intimacy of a church that spent considerable time *"ministering to the Lord and fasting."* The early believers who gathered in Antioch

River Houses Rising

constituted a house church in pursuit of intimacy with God. But, **second**, we also see the supernatural, life changing nature of organic church as the Holy Spirit spoke to these believers with practical things for them to do. This was NOT a *"let's just seek the Lord and enjoy Him"* kind of fellowship. It was a *"let's seek the Lord and listen to what He tells us to do"* kind of church. They were intimate with God, but they were also obedient. Specifically, Paul's first missionary journey began, not with organizing a missions conference, but with an intimate, worshiping church which was *"ministering to the Lord and fasting."* The people of God worshiped and sought Him, the Holy Spirit spoke, and the result was a missions movement that turned the Roman world upside down. That model of spiritual intimacy and supernatural, life changing obedience worked for the New Testament Church. What makes us think it won't work for us today?

Questions For Reflection

Take a moment to reflect on your own spiritual journey. Which best describes your spiritual condition? Spiritual heartburn or spiritual frustration?

Safe Houses of Hope and Prayer represents a practical New Testament response to the "holy discontent" of our generation that combines intimacy with God with obedience to His will.

Chapter 6

The Kingdom In Your House

From that time Jesus began to preach and say, "Repent, for the kingdom of heaven is at hand." (Matthew 4:17)

But He said to them, "I must preach the kingdom of God to the other cities also, for I was sent for this purpose." (Luke 4:43)

"The Kingdom of God is an ocean that an elephant can swim in and a pool that a child can wade in." - Anonymous

The Lost Kingdom

The organized Church has lost the Kingdom of God, and people have begun to notice. Somewhere along the line we traded the mystery, the wonder and the majesty of the Kingdom for a building, or a system of theology or another 40-day purpose driven program. The topic of the Kingdom may occasionally come up in conversation or even receive honorable mention in a sermon, but not because anyone actually takes it seriously anymore. Michael Spencer once observed that Christians today have created a spirituality that wants Jesus on the cover, but not in the book.[18] The same

---

[18] Michael Spencer, ***Mere Churchianity: Finding Your Way Back to Jesus-Shaped Spirituality*** (Colorado Springs: Waterbrook Press, 2010), p. 51.

River Houses Rising

could be said of the Kingdom of God. While the Kingdom may still occasionally appear on the cover of our books, the message, the power, the wonder and the mystery of the Kingdom of God have disappeared from the life of the very Church which owes it's existence to Jesus' proclamation of the Kingdom.

But God wants to change all of that. God wants to place the message, the power and the mystery of the Kingdom back into the hands of those for whom it was intended. God wants to restore the Kingdom of God to your house, and to the Church that meets there. Are you ready to become a "disciple of the Kingdom." [19]

Jesus And The Kingdom

Did you ever notice something. It's sort of subtle, so you might have missed it. But it is very profound. Here it is. Jesus NEVER preached a message on "the Church." In fact, He only mentioned "the Church" twice that we know of (Matthew 16:18; 18:17). But Jesus either referred to or taught on the Kingdom of God over 100 times! I think there's a point there.

Jesus lived and taught the Kingdom of God. It was the heart of His message. Not only did He preach the good news of the

---

[19] We examine the Kingdom of God and what it means to be a disciple of the Kingdom in much greater detail in our book, ***And They Dreamt Of A Kingdom: Biblical Reflections On Discipleship And The Kingdom Of God - Volume 1***, available on our website and from Amazon.com.

The Kingdom In Your House

Kingdom of God, Jesus commanded His disciples to preach the Kingdom: *"And as you go, preach, saying, 'The **kingdom of heaven** is at hand.'"* (Matthew 10:7). To put it differently, followers of Jesus are to be Kingdom-minded disciples with a Kingdom-oriented message. Like Jesus, we don't preach "church." We proclaim a Kingdom. The Kingdom of God.

Because the life, message and ministry of Jesus was all about the Kingdom of God, the good news of the Kingdom of God became the message of the early New Testament Church. How do we know? Well, *first*, we know it because the New Testament talks more about "kingdom" (162 times) than it does about "church" (115 times). That alone should get our undivided attention.

Second, we know this because the disciples themselves preached the Kingdom of God where ever they went: *"But when they believed Philip as he preached good news about the kingdom of God and the name of Jesus Christ, they were baptized, both men and women."* (Acts 8:12) They knew, understood and proclaimed the message of the Kingdom of God. Do we?

Third, we know the Kingdom of God was the message of the early Church because the Apostle Paul - the great Apostle to the Gentiles - made the Kingdom of God his message wherever he went, all the way to Rome: *"He lived there two whole years at his own expense, and welcomed all who came to him, proclaiming the kingdom of God and teaching about the Lord Jesus Christ with all boldness and without*

River Houses Rising

hindrance." (Acts 28:30-31)

When we look at the life of the early Church what we quickly discover is that they didn't *"do evangelism"* as you and I understand it today (You know, *"Have You Heard Of The Four Spiritual Laws?"*). To our knowledge they never led anyone in a "sinner's prayer," never challenged anyone to "ask Jesus in their hearts," and never encouraged anyone to join the church. Rather, they proclaimed the Kingdom, they taught the Kingdom and they lived the Kingdom. And people around them responded in faith to the message of the Kingdom of God which they both heard and saw manifested in the lives of these Kingdom-oriented believers.

What Is The Kingdom of God?

If Jesus and the early Christian believers proclaimed the Kingdom of God, it might be worthwhile for us to take a few minutes to define what we mean. What is the Kingdom of God and what does it have to do with organic house church?

Simply put, the Kingdom of God is the dynamic reign and kingly rule of God, irrespective of people or places. God is King and rules His universe, regardless of time or location. On five different occasions the Scriptures sum up God's Kingly reign by simply declaring, *"The Lord reigns!"* (See 1 Chronicles 16:31; Psalm 93:1; Psalm 96:10; 97:1; 99:1). The Kingdom of God consists of this simple reality: God reigns as Lord and King.

The Kingdom In Your House

1. The Kingdom of God - God's Kingly Rule - Is At the Heart of the Biblical Message. Consider this passage from the Psalms:

"All your works shall give thanks to you, O LORD, and all your saints shall bless you! They shall speak of the glory of your kingdom and tell of your power, to make known to the children of man your mighty deeds, and the glorious splendor of your kingdom. Your kingdom is an everlasting kingdom, and your dominion endures throughout all generations." (Psalms 145:10-13)

The people of God have always known and understood something about the Kingdom of God, as this passage from the Old Testament clearly demonstrates. They understood that God's kingly rule - His dominion - knows no boundaries of space or time. It is "everlasting" whether we look backward through eternity past, or whether we look forward into eternity future. God's Kingdom - His dominion - is both majestic and everlasting, whether seen from the Old Testament or from the New Testament. And His Kingdom is manifested and established whenever an individual acknowledges His Lordship and by faith submits their will and their lives to His Kingly rule.

2. Jesus brought the Kingdom and Promised the Kingdom. The message of the Old Testament was that God would one day establish His Kingdom - His kingly rule - on earth. God's enemies would be crushed while injustice, hunger, disease and even death itself would be destroyed.

River Houses Rising

And all men would come under the Kingly rule of God in the person of His "anointed one" or "Messiah." It was this as-yet-unfulfilled promise of a coming "Messianic Kingdom" led by a Messiah-King which hung in the air when Jesus came to Israel proclaiming, *"Repent, for the kingdom of heaven is at hand."*

The Kingdom of God was indeed at hand. It had arrived in the person of the Messiah-King - Jesus - God's Anointed One. But He had come, not to crush the Roman enemies of God's people, but to manifest the reality and the power of God's Kingly Rule. He demonstrated His Kingly rule over disease by healing the sick, the lame and the blind. He demonstrated His Kingly rule over the demonic spiritual realm by casting out demons and delivering those bound by demonic oppression. He demonstrated His Kingly rule over creation itself by changing water to wine and stilling storms with a word. He demonstrated His power to eliminate hunger in the Kingdom of God by multiplying fish and bread. And he demonstrated His power over sin and death by raising people from the dead, and by rising from the grave Himself.

But the arrival of the Kingdom in all its fulness would remain a promise for a future day when the risen and ascended Jesus would return at the end of this present evil age, separate the sheep from the goats, judge all men for what they had done with the message of the Kingdom, and establish His Kingdom on earth in all its fulness with Jesus as Messiah-King over all.

The Kingdom In Your House

3. The Kingdom Creates the Church, Not the Other Way Around. The organized Church of our day often forgets that Jesus preached the Kingdom, not the Church. Jesus declared that the Kingdom of God was at hand, not that the Church was at hand.

The Kingdom of God is the greater whole of which the Church is the lesser part. You and I must first be "born again" into the Kingdom of God (John 3:3-7) before we can assemble together with other born again believers as the Church. The Church is created when individuals like you and me respond in faith to the message of the Kingdom. By faith we acknowledge, confess and repent of our sins, asking God's forgiveness based upon the sacrificial death of Jesus for our sins. We exercise faith in Jesus the Messiah-King as our savior from sin and death. In humility and faith we submit to His Kingly rule in our lives and become life-long *"disciples of the Kingdom,"* living lives of obedience and faith. When we gather together with other such believers we constitute the Church, a manifestation of the Kingdom of God in a still-fallen and lost world.

4. The Church is not the Kingdom, but is God's witness of His Kingdom to an unbelieving world. The calling of the Church is not to proclaim or exalt itself, or even to urge others to join the church. Rather, as Kingdom minded and Kingdom oriented disciples our calling is to bear personal witness to the reality of the Kingdom of God, just as Jesus told the disciples, *"And this gospel of the kingdom shall be preached in the whole world for a witness to all the nations,*

River Houses Rising

and then the end shall come" (Matthew 24:14). Everything the present unbelieving world will ever know about the Kingdom of God it will learn through the witness of the Church, specifically through the Church which meets in your house.

5. The Church Is the Instrument of the Kingdom. While the fulness of the Kingdom of God remains a future promise, it is through His Church that Jesus continues His mission of proclaiming, revealing, teaching and demonstrating the Kingdom of God. One day - hopefully very soon - His Kingdom will come and His will shall be done on earth just as it is in heaven. That's His promise. But until that day arrives (at the end of the Age when Jesus establishes His Kingdom on earth) the Church is His instrument here and now to manifest His Kingdom to the world. The Church is the instrument for the message of the Kingdom, a message which has not changed since Jesus proclaimed it: *"Repent, for the kingdom of heaven is at hand."* The Church is also the instrument for the power of the Kingdom of God, what Scripture refers to as *"the powers of the Age to Come."* The power of the Kingdom of God is seen and experienced as the Church prays for people to be set free from the power of sin (salvation), from sickness and disease (healing), from demonic oppression (deliverance) and even from death itself (end-time resurrection). And the Church is the instrument for revealing the mysteries of the Kingdom as it teaches the truths of Scripture (Matthew 13:11). And the Church is the instrument for manifesting the love, mercy and kindness of the Kingdom through good deeds done in the name of Jesus,

The Kingdom In Your House

the King.

House Churches Bridge Two Worlds

As the illustration below seeks to show, organic house churches function as a bridge between two worlds or "ages."

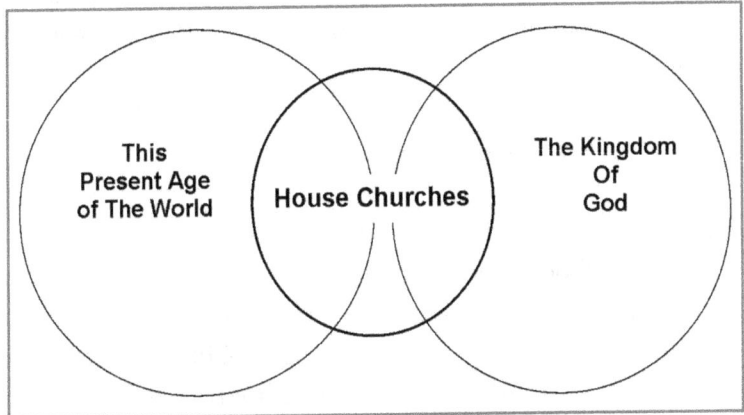

House Churches are a bridge between "This Present Evil Age" and The Kingdom of God in "The Age To Come"

The Scriptures refer to this world in which we currently live as *"this present evil age"* (Galatians 1:4) or as *"the present age"* (Mark 10:30; Titus 2:12). But the fullness of the Kingdom of God belongs to what the Scriptures refer to as *"the age to come"* (again, see Mark 10:30; Matthew 12:32). And between these two "ages" stands the Church (and more specifically in our illustration, organic house churches). It is in the organic house church in your *Safe House of Hope And Prayer* where your friends, your neighbors and others who are seeking spiritual truth will encounter the reality of the Kingdom of God

River Houses Rising

and *"the powers of the age to come."* (Hebrews 6:5) There they will experience the reality of God's Presence in a community of believers. There they will experience the reality of forgiveness, the reality of answered prayer, the reality of healing from sickness and disease, the reality of deliverance from demonic bondages and more. In short, it is in the Church that meets in your house where they will touch, taste and experience the reality of the Kingdom of God - and be forever changed by it.

The Kingdom Restored To Your House

If the bad news is that the Church of our day has lost the Kingdom of God, then the good news is that God is restoring it. The even better news is that He wants to restore the Kingdom of God to your house and to the Church with meets there. The greatest, most profound manifestation of the Kingdom of God that your friends and neighbors will ever see will be what they see take place in your house church.

Questions For Reflection

Reflecting on this Chapter, what did you discover about the Kingdom and the Church that you did not know before.

Safe Houses of Hope And Prayer represent nothing less than a bridge between two worlds and a practical manifestation of the Kingdom of God in your house.

Chapter 7

"River Houses"

In the previous chapter we examined the relationship between organic house churches and the Kingdom of God. We saw how organic house churches function as a bridge between the world of this present age and the future world of the age to come and the fulness of the Kingdom of God. As a bridge between these two worlds, organic house churches play a key role in accomplishing God's three great purposes.

It has always been the heart of God to do three things: 1) to build His Kingdom, 2) to call out a people to Himself, and 3) to pour out the River of His Spirit. In our day, I believe God is raising up a new-but-old biblical vessel in the form of organic house churches to accomplish His three great purposes. Can you hear what He is saying? Others are hearing it.

Not too long ago one of the mature prophetic people in our house church network had a conversation with a Christian couple who are gifted prophetic intercessors (they also attend a local megachurch). *"What are these 'river houses' I keep hearing from the Holy Spirit?"* she asked my friend. When I heard about the conversation I couldn't help but laugh. For some time the Lord had been telling me that the coming move of His Spirit would be an outpouring of the River of His Spirit in great power which would flow through organic house churches. She heard the Holy Spirit describe

River Houses Rising

them as *"river houses."* We are now entering the season of "River Houses Rising" when a flood-tide of God's Spirit is going to flow through these new-but-old channels which we are calling *Safe Houses of Hope And Prayer*, organic house churches meeting in homes like yours.

What she heard confirmed what I had been hearing and teaching, and am now sharing with you. The River of God's Spirit is about to flow in great power and blessing, and organic house churches are the new-but-old channels through which He plans to flow. And He wants to flow through your house.

What Is A Safe House of Hope And Prayer?

The concept for *Safe Houses of Hope And Prayer* was originally born out of our work in the West Central neighborhood of Spokane, one of the poorest, toughest, drug-infested and dysfunctional neighborhoods in our city. After months of feeding 150-to-200 (and as many as 300!) people in the front yard of a neighborhood house, leading Bible studies, working with children, drug dealers, drug users, domestic violence, families in crisis and much more, God gave birth to the idea of *Safe Houses of Hope And Prayer*. He opened our eyes to see the obvious. We had, in fact, become a *Safe House of Hope And Prayer* - a neighborhood organic house church - where people from the neighborhood could come and experience God's love among a community of believers who were willing to reach out in love to those around them. The concept of *Safe Houses of*

"River Houses"

Hope And Prayer rests upon our practical experience of taking the Kingdom of God into homes and neighborhoods with power to transform them, believing that there is no need so great or overwhelming that the Kingdom of God cannot meet and overcome it.

It is probably safe to say that most people in our Postmodern culture have never witnessed or experienced a genuine, authentic expression of the Kingdom of God either in the Church or in their neighborhoods. This is your opportunity to change that. This is your opportunity to introduce people to an authentic experience of the Kingdom of God right where they live . . . in their homes.

A Safe House Of Hope And Prayer Is . . .

A *Safe House of Hope And Prayer* is many things. Unfortunately we only have time and space to mention a few of them. The list that follows is NOT exhaustive. Hopefully it is simply enough to whet your appetite for more! And in reality, you ARE the "more." What happens from this point forward is really up to you!

An organic house church living, growing and meeting in your house! Let's talk about this for just a moment. What does it mean to be "organic"?[20] What we mean is that the

---

[20] For more about the nature of organic growth, see *"Lesson 40 - The Organic Growth Of The Kingdom"* in our book, ***And They Dreamt Of A Kingdom***, available on our website from Amazon.com.

River Houses Rising

church of Jesus is not a building or an institution. Jesus isn't planning to return for a betrothed building or an organization. Jesus isn't coming back for the denominational HQ! He is returning for a betrothed bride that we refer to as the Church! The Church of Jesus is an ORGANISM; one that is alive and growing! The question is, *"Is it alive and growing in your house?"*! Jesus even described the Kingdom of God (of which the Church is a local manifestation) in organic terms:

"He put another parable before them, saying, 'The kingdom of heaven is like a grain of mustard seed that a man took and sowed in his field. It is the smallest of all seeds, but when it has grown it is larger than all the garden plants and becomes a tree, so that the birds of the air come and make nests in its branches.' He told them another parable. 'The kingdom of heaven is like leaven that a woman took and hid in three measures of flour, till it was all leavened.'"(Matthew 13:31-33)

Do you see it? Like the Kingdom of which it is a part, house church is organic. It is an ORGANISM, one that is alive and growing, like Mustard trees and bread yeast! The real question is this: *"Is it alive and growing in your house?"*!

A Safe Place To Heal - People today are in need of various kinds of healing, and that includes emotional and spiritual healing from wounds received at the hands of the Church as they have known and experienced it. Studies done by The Barna Group indicate that nearly 65 million Americans have not attended church within the past 6 months. They are the "unchurched." Many of them (some 61%) identify themselves

"River Houses"

as Christians. Further studies suggest that 37% (or 24 million) of those people who have stopped attending church said they avoid churches because of negative past experiences in churches or with church people. In other words, they are the "walking wounded" who regard the traditional institutional church as the place where they were wounded in the name of God by professing believers. The good news is that we worship a God who *"heals the brokenhearted, And binds up their wounds"* (Psalm 147:3), and the organic house church is an ideal place for that healing to take place.

In addition to emotional and spiritual healing, the organic house church is also a place of frequent physical healing. In our own house church we have seen profound physical healings take place in the lives of numerous people. And we are not alone. My friend Jim Rutz is a pioneer of the organic house church movement in America, starting with his book, **The Open Church**. When Jim isn't traveling and teaching simple church around the world he is part of an organic house church in Colorado Springs. Jim's simple house church of around 20 people reaches out to anyone needing physical healing or deliverance from spiritual oppressions of various sorts. In one recent six-month period they saw God heal numerous conditions, many of which were considered incurable. These included cancers of the liver, prostate, and pituitary, two severe cases of osteonecrosis (disintegrated jawbones), lupus, type 1 juvenile onset diabetes, post-polio syndrome, multiple sclerosis, arthritis, scleroderma, and more. *"We're very ordinary folks,"* Jim commented, *"no*

River Houses Rising

professionals, no pastors, no shouting, and no collections whatsoever. But we do offer quiet, open meetings about once a month in Colorado Springs. We don't hit 100%, and we've still got our training wheels on, but we're improving." [21] That's the healing potential of simple house church.

A Safe Place To Experience Truth - The reality of God's healing power and presence in organic house churches highlights another important characteristic, namely, experiential truth. Organic house church offers people both a safe place and an opportunity to "come and see" (John 1:46). It is a place where people can eat together, pray together, share life's struggles together and experience God's grace and power together (hmm, just like Jesus and His disciples did!). To use one of my favorite illustrations, in house church we *bake* bread together, we *break* bread together and we *eat* bread together. And the truth of that bread is experiential, not theoretical.

A Place For Mutual Ministry - Organic house church isn't about what the Pastor has to share. It's about what YOU have to share. The Apostle Paul described it this way: *"What then, brothers? When you come together, each one has a hymn, a lesson, a revelation, a tongue, or an interpretation. Let all things be done for building up."* (1 Corinthians 14:26) Did you hear what he said? When the house church there in the Greek city of Corinth assembled together, each one - that

---

[21] From personal e-mail correspondence with my friend, Jim. Used by permission.

"River Houses"

is, each person - was to bring something to share with the Church. And the result of this kind of mutual ministry is the building up (or "edification" - Greek: <u>*oikodomeo*</u>) of the body. The spiritual building of the Church is built up with living stones when everyone participates and ministers by bringing what God has given them (him or her)!

A Place For Good Deeds - Take just a moment and consider what Jesus had to say about "good deeds" (and, yes, there will be a quiz, so pay attention!):

"You are the light of the world. A city set on a hill cannot be hidden. Nor do people light a lamp and put it under a basket, but on a stand, and it gives light to all in the house. In the same way, let your light shine before others, so that they may see your good works and give glory to your Father who is in heaven." (Matthew 5:14-16)

O.K., here's the quiz: How did Jesus say your "light" (i.e., the light of Jesus in you) would shine and be seen? Answer: Through your "good deeds." So, where are your good deeds?

The reality is that our world thinks it can manifest good deeds without Jesus, while the Church thinks it can manifest Jesus without good deeds. The world's plan seems to be working better than the Church's plan. This really shouldn't surprise us since the New Testament talks about the importance of good deeds in the life of the believer nearly 30 different

River Houses Rising

times. A believer without good deeds is a faith without fruit.[22]

We once did a Thanksgiving outreach for a local elementary school. I explained to our volunteers who were helping that *"Sometimes the Kingdom of God tastes like turkey and dressing."* And that's what good deeds by believers do; they communicate the goodness of the Kingdom of God in terms that people understand. Organic house church represents an opportunity for believers to personally serve those around them through good deeds. And there are many different ways this can be done (we discuss a few of these in our book, ***The Least of These***). Once, as part of an outreach in a low-income neighborhood, we contacted three local supermarkets and arranged to pick up their day-old bread and pastries which we distributed throughout the neighborhood to people in need. Why? Because sometimes the Kingdom of God tastes like day-old pastries.

Look for opportunities to serve others in simple ways like picking up trash on their lawn, moving their empty garbage can up to their house if they are still gone late in the day, putting their paper up by their door if they are away. If a neighbor is struggling financially, hold a yard sale and use the proceeds to help meet that need. Look for an unmet need and meet it. Use your imagination.

---

[22]This issue of "good deeds" is so important in the life of the believer that we have written a book on the subject entitled, ***The Least of These: The Role of Good Deeds In A Jesus Shaped Spirituality.*** It is available on our website from Amazon.com.

"River Houses"

A Place for Building Relationships and Community - Imagine for just a moment that you attend a local megachurch of 2,000 people. How many of those people do you know beyond their name and saying "hello" on Sunday morning? If you do the mental math you'll discover that you really don't know more than about 20 people on any close basis (their struggles, their fears, their spiritual depth or spiritual goals). In other words, your circle of close relationships and community is about the size of a house church. It's impossible to have any genuine sense of biblical community with 2,000 people (or 200 people for that matter).

Through years of outreaches and house church functions we have been amazed to discover the relationships and sense of community that can be built over the informal atmosphere of a potluck and bible study in someone's living room. We discovered that people have life-stories to tell, including their spiritual journeys, and often times they are simply looking for someone who cares enough to listen to their story with love and without judgmentalism.

A Place For Discovering A Jesus-Shaped Spirituality - At the risk of teasing you, we'll save this one for the next Chapter (consider yourself duly teased!).

A New Channel for the River of God's Spirit - There is a growing chorus of Christians today who are fasting and praying for revival. Predicting and prophesying a coming revival has become a cottage industry today. But if God should graciously and powerfully answer all of our prayers for

River Houses Rising

revival, are we prepared to receive it? How and where will this "river of revival" flow, since only about 26% of Americans presently attend Church? Where are the vessels to receive this outpouring and its fruit? I believe that the rise of organic house churches - *Safe Houses of Hope And Prayer* - represent the new wineskin for what God is about to do. The River of God's Spirit is preparing to flow in unprecedented power for spiritual revival, renewal and community transformation. The result will be tens of thousands of people who will be swept into the Kingdom of God and they will find their spiritual homes in organic house churches. The only question remaining question is, *"Will your house be one of them"*?!

Questions For Reflection

Reflecting on this Chapter, what did you learn about what it means to be an organic house church that you did not know before? How does this encourage you to become a *Safe House of Hope And Prayer*?

Safe Houses of Hope And Prayer represent the new wineskin for what God is about to do, an organic house church meeting in your house.

Chapter 8

Pursuing A Jesus-Shaped Spirituality

In the previous chapter we began to define what we mean by organic house church and *Safe Houses of Hope and Prayer*. Much of that definition or description had little to do with structure (We'll have more to say about structure in Chapter 9). Why? Because while structure is good and important, it is NEVER enough. Bill Beckham, an internationally recognized leader in the cell church movement, once observed,

"You never change a structure until you change a value. We do not transplant systems and structures. We transplant values and life."

Changing a structure, such as moving your "venue" from a big church building to smaller personal homes or even public coffee shops, won't solve any spiritual problems of the heart. That's because where ever we go we take our spiritual problems with us. It's what I call our "spiritual baggage," and like Christian versions of Jacob Marley in *"A Christmas Carol"* we drag our spiritual baggage with us wherever we go - clanging all the way. So, in addition to changing our location, we also need to change our values by examining our hearts.

For several years I was part of a regular e-mail chat group with numerous pastors and leaders about ministry in the

River Houses Rising

Church. There was one particular e-mail which I still remember, because it had a profound impact on me (profound enough that I can still remember the writer's point). The author of that e-mail made a simple point that went as follows: *"The main thing is to always remember to keep the main thing the main thing."*

So, let me ask you. When it comes to church and spirituality, what in your opinion is *"the main thing"*? Your answer to that question will begin to reveal the true nature of your spiritual baggage; the spiritual values which you will carry with you into organic house church. While Charles Dickens offered no hope for Jacob Marley, the good news is that there is hope for you. It is possible to shed your baggage and to change your values.

The Things That Shape Us

We are all shaped by something. Some of those things are beyond our control, like the genetics we received from our parents. Others are choices we make, like opinions and attitudes we hear from others and adopt as our own. When it comes to matters involving our "spirituality" - how we understand such things as God, faith, obedience, etc. - we are generally shaped by one of two things: religion or relationship. This is as true for you and me as it was for

Pursuing A Jesus-Shaped Spirituality

Jesus' first disciples. [23]

Jesus Versus The Disciples

When Jesus first called His disciples, they were men with a deeply ingrained religion-shaped spirituality. Nearly everything they thought they knew about the God of Israel they had learned from the institutional religious structure of official 1st Century Judaism. And it showed. They regarded all gentiles (non-Jews) as "unclean" and refused to associate with them (Acts 10:28), because that's what Judaism taught. They particularly hated the Samaritans (John Chapter 4). They regarded them as religious half-breeds and were ready on a moment's notice to call down fire from heaven to consume them (Luke 9:52-54). Their religion-shaped spirituality told them to avoid all gentiles, most women (outside of family members), lepers, tax-collectors in particular and "sinners" in general. It was a sin to heal anyone on the Sabbath, and a man was probably born blind because either he or his parents had sinned (John 9:2). According to what they had been taught, God was a legalist, and so were they. To these followers of a religion-shaped spirituality one could not be truly spiritual or religious without obeying the more than 5,000 religious rules and regulations which governed institutional Judaism.

---

[23] My thanks to the late Michael Spencer for challenging my thinking on the issue of a Jesus-shaped spirituality. See ***Mere Churchianity: Finding Your Way Back to Jesus-Shaped Spirituality*** (Colorado Springs: Waterbrook Press, 2010).

River Houses Rising

Then they met Jesus. And for the next three-and-a-half years He would shake their religious spirituality to the breaking point. As they traveled with Him along the highways and byways of Judea, they watched in stunned disbelief as He ministered to both women AND Samaritans, and allowed a woman of questionable character ("a sinner") to minister to Him (Luke 7:36-39). They watched Him heal lepers with a touch, when a spoken word would have accomplished the same thing, and they even joined Him as He dined in their homes (Matthew 26:6) because He wanted to make a point. They followed Him as He dined in the homes of tax-collectors, "hung out" with assorted "sinners" and ministered to a gentile woman and her daughter (Matthew 15:22-28). They watched as He healed on the Sabbath to provoke a confrontation with the religious rulers of institutional Judaism (Matthew 12:10; Mark 3:2; Luke 14:3). There was more, but you get the point.

For three-and-a-half years Jesus challenged everything His disciples knew about God, faith, religion and spirituality. Jesus challenged their view of God until He was their view of God. He challenged their view of religious authority until He was their view of religious authority. He challenged their understanding of obedience to God until they understood that obedience to Him WAS obedience to God. And He challenged their view of spirituality and religion until He WAS their view of spirituality and religion. He challenged them to rid themselves of any and all other things in their spiritual lives until He and He alone was *"the main thing"* in their spiritual lives.

Pursuing A Jesus-Shaped Spirituality

Twelve Changed Men

After spending three-and-a-half years with Jesus, the disciples emerged from the events of the crucifixion and resurrection as profoundly changed men. Scripture recognizes and points out this profound change. Two examples will make our point. The **first** example is found early in the Book of Acts. In their first post-resurrection encounter with the disciples, the Jewish religious authorities could not figure out who these people were until they *"began to recognize them as having been with Jesus."* (Acts 4:13) The disciples had been changed beyond recognition. They were no longer the obedient Jewish religionists Jesus had first called along the shores of Galilee. They were now men who had been profoundly transformed by a Jesus-shaped spirituality and who could no longer live by the old religious rules.

The **second** example of the profound change in the disciples occurs in the city of Antioch where we read, *"and the disciples were first called Christians in Antioch"* (Acts 11:26). In the Greek, the word "Christians" is what we call a *diminutive* - a word formed by adding a suffix to a root word in order to indicate "smallness." The Greek term "Christians" literally means "little Christ-ones." We don't know who first referred to the disciples in Antioch as Christians in Acts 11. I suspect it was people outside the Church who intended the label as something approaching a slur. If so, they unwittingly paid those early disciples the highest possible compliment. They accused them of looking like Jesus. They accused

River Houses Rising

them of manifesting a Jesus-shaped spirituality.

Today, we are very loose with our terminology. We describe someone as a Christian simply because they attend a church service and make some nominal profession of faith. Our standards are really pretty low. Not so in the early church. "Christian" was the label given by unbelievers who watched the early disciples as they manifested a Jesus-shaped spirituality in their daily lives, and in the face of mounting persecution. The disciples now looked more like Jesus than like Jewish religionists. To state it another way that is meaningful to us today, *"A Christian is a disciple who manifests a Jesus-shaped spirituality."*

So, Who Do You Look Like?

At the end of the day you and I are the embodiment of what we believe and the things which have shaped us. We are either the living embodiment of a set of religious rules and beliefs given to us by the religious institutions which have shaped us, or we are the embodiment of a daily relationship with the living, risen Jesus. We are either disciples of the Kingdom of God and its values or we are disciples of a religious organization and its rules.

What is a Jesus-shaped spirituality? It is the life of a disciple who looks like Jesus and who sounds like the Kingdom of God rather than looking and sounding like a religious leader and his (or her) organization. A Jesus-shaped spirituality is one which challenges us to become disciples of the Kingdom

Pursuing A Jesus-Shaped Spirituality

by submitting our lives to the Lordship of Jesus, the Messiah-King, and to follow him in daily obedience. A Jesus-shaped spirituality means we become genuine followers rather than occasional fans of the One who claimed to be God-incarnate. Followers of Jesus seek to obey Him daily, as opposed to fans who are satisfied with a weekly pep rally.

Church attendance in America has fallen dramatically in recent years, from 42% of adults in 1965 to around 20% of the adult population on any given Sunday today.[24] People in our culture are walking away from traditional organizational forms of church and the religion-based spirituality it offers. Could it be because what they have seen simply doesn't resemble the movement Jesus started or the process Jesus Himself used to make disciples?

Jesus wants to be *"the main thing"* in everything we do. He wants to challenge our view of God until He IS our view of God. Jesus wants to challenge our view of spirituality until He IS our view of spirituality. He wants to challenge our view of church until He IS our view of church. And He wants to challenge us to rid ourselves of other things until He and He alone is *"the main thing."*

Quo Vadis, Dominus

The pursuit of a Jesus-shaped spirituality often means

---

[24]See our earlier comments on this topic along with the accompanying footnotes in Chapter 4.

River Houses Rising

cutting our ties with the comfortable and safe religious traditions, customs and assumptions we have known, and embracing the wildness of the Kingdom of God as proclaimed by an itinerant rabbi and carpenter from Nazareth Who now rules it as Messiah and King. The religion-shaped spirituality you may have known in the past is not a reliable guide to who Jesus is, or what He wants you to do today. A Jesus-shaped spirituality must be pursued on Jesus' terms and no others. That was the first lesson Jesus' disciples had to learn, and it is a lesson we need to learn (again) as well.

One of my favorite old movies is the 1951 epic, *"Quo Vadis."* Done in typical over-the-top Hollywood fashion, it is still a good watch and worth a couple of hours and a bucket of popcorn. It is the story of Christians and the beginnings of persecution under the Roman Emperor Nero. Late in the movie, as Christians in Rome are being rounded up and led to their deaths in the arena, there is a scene involving the character, Peter. He is on a trip away from Rome when he senses that there is something wrong and he ponders whether he should continue on or return to Rome. As he ponders what to do, he prays aloud (in Latin, of course!), *"Quo vadis, Dominus,"* which loosely translates, *"Where are you going, Lord?"* (sorry, I won't spoil the moment by telling you what happens!).

"Where are you going, Lord?" is the prayer of a *"disciple of the Kingdom"* in pursuit of a Jesus-shaped spirituality. It isn't about where the church or denomination is going. It isn't about the awesome vision of the pastor, the deacons, the

Pursuing A Jesus-Shaped Spirituality

elders, the presbytery, that visiting speaker who has a plan to win the world for Jesus, or anyone else for that matter. Those things can have an important place, but they can never take the place of the disciple who daily asks, *"Where are you going, Lord?"* and then follows in obedience and faith. As Michael Spencer rightly observed, life as a Jesus-follower grows out of Jesus and the gospel, not out of the Church.[25] While the Church can be a valuable resource for our spiritual development, the Church is not Christ or the Kingdom. And for these reasons alone, the Church can never be the ultimate source of a person's life with God.

Organic House Church And Discipleship

Someone once said, *"Disciples make Churches. Churches don't make disciples."* I want to explain why this statement is false, before I explain why it is true (yes, it is both). Contrary to this observation, Churches do, in fact, make disciples. Religious organizations, including institutional Churches, produce "disciples" whose spirituality reflects the religious attitudes, rules, beliefs, practices, behaviors and programs of that institution. Religious organizations produce "disciples" who manifest a religion-shaped spirituality. It was true of the institutional Judaism of Jesus's day, and it has been true throughout the history of the Church.

But it is also true that disciples make Churches. As someone recently observed, *"If you make disciples, you will get*

---

[25]Spencer, ***Mere Churchianity***, p. 152.

River Houses Rising

Churches; but if you plant churches you may or may not get disciples." I understand what this person meant. Followers of Jesus who are disciples of His Kingdom in pursuit of a Jesus-shaped spirituality will gather together with other like-minded believers and will form Churches - local manifestations of the Kingdom of God. And we believe that many of them will gather as organic house churches. The only remaining question is this. Which kind of disciple are you, and which kind of disciple do you want to reproduce? [26]

So, What Is The Main Thing?

We are now back to the question which we posed at the outset of this Chapter. Do you remember the e-mail point that started this discussion: *"The main thing is to always remember to keep the main thing the main thing."* When it comes to matters of faith, church and spirituality, what is *"the main thing"*?

By now the answer should be obvious. As the chart on the following page illustrates, in the early New Testament Church the main thing was Jesus, particularly in His resurrection power and glory. Their message was that the Kingdom of God had come, the Resurrection of Jesus was the proof, and the outpouring of the Spirit was the sign and seal that they

---

[26] Again, for a more thorough treatment of the nature of biblical discipleship, see our book ***And They Dreamt Of A Kingdom: Biblical Reflections On Discipleship And The Kingdom of God - Volume 1***, available on our website from Amazon.com.

Pursuing A Jesus-Shaped Spirituality

were indeed living in the "last days" as promised by the prophet Joel.

How The Early Church Kept *"The Main Thing"* The Main Thing
Peter at Pentecost - Acts 2:14-40
Peter In The Temple - Acts 3:12-26
Peter to Sanhedrin - Acts 4:5-12
Peter to Council - Acts 5:29-32
Stephen to Sanhedrin - Acts 7
Peter to Cornelius - Acts 10:34-43
Peter to Church in Jerusalem - Acts 11:4-17
Paul in Synagogue at Pisidian Antioch - Acts 13:16-41
Peter to Jerusalem - Council Acts 15:6-11
James To Jerusalem - Council Acts 15:13-21
Paul on Mars Hill in Athens - Acts 17:22-31
Paul to Ephesian Elders - Acts 20:17-35
Paul to Jews in Jerusalem - Acts 22:1-21
Paul to Sanhedrin - Acts 23:1-6
Paul Before Felix - Acts 24:10-21
Paul Before King Agrippa - Acts 26:1-23
Paul to Jewish Leaders at Rome - Acts 28:23-29

River Houses Rising

The chart on the previous page shows 17 sermons from the book of Acts. When you examine these 17 sermons, "the main thing" is quickly apparent. When the 11 Apostles chose a replacement for Judas the specific mandate was that this person *"should become a witness with us of His resurrection."* The resurrected Jesus was "the main thing." The power promised to the waiting Church in Acts 1:8 was power to be His witnesses. And that witness was specifically a witness to the resurrected, living Jesus. On six different occasions we are told that the early church was a witness to the events surrounding the resurrected Christ (See Acts 1:22; 2:32; 3:15; 5:32; 10:39-41, 13:30-31). And the resurrection of Jesus is mentioned some 19 times in the preaching and ministry of the early church. Without the resurrected, living and exalted Jesus everything else falls apart, and our faith is in vain (see 1 Corinthians 15).

Given these realities, it should come as no surprise that Jesus Himself placed His death and resurrection at the heart of every gathering of believers by commanding a specific act to be observed when we gather. Remember? We refer to it as the Lord's Supper. Paul tells us in 1 Corinthians 11:26 that, *"For as often as you eat this bread and drink the cup, you proclaim the Lord's death until He comes."* This is why, whenever I lead a celebration of the Lord's Table, I usually read Paul's words from 1 Corinthians 11:23-26. I do this, not because I can't think of anything else to do, but because scripturally and practically it brings our focus back to *"the main thing."* Jesus' death and resurrection is the main thing; it is the center of all we do. Everything else (i.e., power for

Pursuing A Jesus-Shaped Spirituality

ministry, spiritual gifts, evangelism, etc.) flows from the resurrection power of our Lord Jesus Christ as it is poured out upon His worshiping church.

And "church" is simply the gathering of those individuals who by faith are *"disciples of the Kingdom"* in pursuit of a Jesus-shaped spirituality. Organic house church is the gathering of disciples who look like Jesus and who sound like the Kingdom of God. The further any individual or group gets away from Jesus and the Kingdom of God in the pursuit of other things - even good things - the more they will look like, sound like and act like another religious organization.

Questions For Reflection

What is the difference between a Jesus-shaped spirituality and a religion-shaped spirituality?

Which of these two "spiritualities" best describes you? Why?

Safe Houses of Hope And Prayer represent the pursuit of values over structure, the pursuit of organic house churches where Jesus is *"the main thing"* and where Kingdom-minded believers can pursue a Jesus-shaped spirituality in the company of other *"disciples of the Kingdom."*

River Houses Rising

Chapter 9

It's Time To "Just Do It"

O.K., as my fishermen friends like to say, *"It's time to fish or cut bait."* It's time to move from theory to practice. At this point I am tempted to encourage you to go back and re-read Chapter 2, *"The Bucket That Rube Built."* Why? Because most of us have in our minds a picture of Christian spirituality and church that is far more religious and complicated than the reality of organic house church. This means that our natural tendency will be to over engineer everything we do, when in reality we need to keep things very simple. That's why I want to urge you to become *"The First Church of Those Who 'Just Do It!'"*

"Just Do It!"

When it comes to organic house church, there really is no right or wrong way to *"Just Do It."* For example, my wife and I actually started doing house church in a Mexican restaurant. At that time I was doing a weekly radio program, talking about house church on a local Christian station. It aired on Saturday mornings. At the end of each program I invited listeners to come and join us for "dinner and house church" at a small Mexican restaurant. A couple of people came the first night, more the second night, and before long we had as many as 50 people packed into the back room of the restaurant. We talked about life, shared things God had

River Houses Rising

shown us during the week, sometimes sharing a brief devotional thought, prayed together and for each other, and left with a sense that God had been with us. Here's my point. Each of us needs to discover what works for our particular situation to bring people together in our home or office, or dorm room, or even in a Mexican restaurant! We each need to discover how to *Just Do It!*

My friend Neil Cole did a talk at a National House Church Conference entitled *"Drink Coffee, Play Chess and Listen."* He told about going to secular coffee houses, drinking coffee, playing chess with people, listening to their stories and inviting them to his house for dinner. He said it wasn't long before he had a living room full of people talking about Jesus. That is profoundly simple, and simply profound!

My friend John White of Denver (www.lk10.com) likes simple approaches to organic church. He teaches what he calls "CO2" which stands for "Churches Of Two." This is two believers gathering together for mutual support and encouragement. Is it possible for organic church to be that simple? Yes, it can!

Welcome to simple organic house church and *"The First Church of Those Who 'Just Do It'"*!

Organic house church, what we are calling *Safe Houses of Hope And Prayer,* is not a program. It is a Spirit-birthed lifestyle of "being the church" in our homes and neighborhoods. Our motto is, *"We don't "go to church, we are*

It's Time To "Just Do It"

the Church" (and so are you!). The goal is to turn our homes into authentic bridges between the Kingdom of God we all know and love and the lost world of this present age where our friends, neighbors and co-workers live and work. Our mandate as followers of Christ is to shine where God has placed us as lights to a lost and dying world.

People today may be abandoning organized forms of "church" as they have known and experienced it, but they are still seeking moral and spiritual direction. As author A. W. Tozer repeated points out, God has made us to worship, and we WILL worship, even if it means that people will worship the wrong things.[27] They are adrift in a sea of darkness and need a safe place of hope and prayer where they can discover a personal and authentic relationship with Jesus Christ. Often, people in our Postmodern culture are expressing their need and hunger in a new way. They are saying *"God, yes! Church, no!"* If that offends you, get over it. They have. It's your problem, not theirs. *Safe Houses of Hope And Prayer* provide a practical response to this cry of our generation. A *Safe House of Hope And Prayer* is a personal bridge for the Kingdom of God in the heart of your neighborhood where we as Christians can model what it means to BE the Church.

---

[27] A. W. Tozer, ***The Purpose of Man: Designed To Worship,*** Compiled and Edited by James L. Snyder (Ventura, CA: Regal, 2009).

River Houses Rising

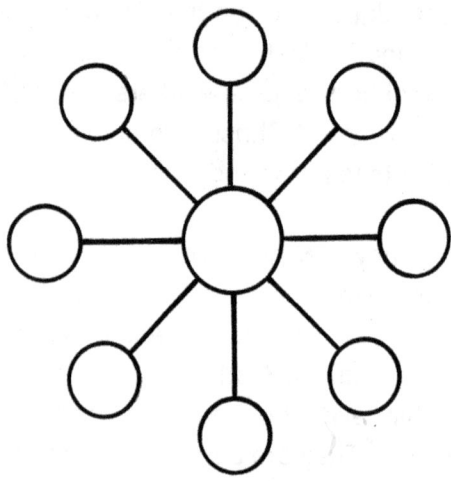

A Simple Way To Begin

So, where do we start? How do we become consciously intentional and actually begin the process (or better yet, the adventure) of becoming not just an organic house church but a growing and multiplying house church? At the risk of being accused of "over engineering" things, I want to offer an illustration for your use and consideration. The purpose is to graphically illustrate what your house church might look like. It might look something like the diagram above. The concept is really pretty simple, so we'll take it in simple steps.

Make a Personal Commitment - Look at the above diagram. Begin by placing yourself in the center circle. That's right, write your name in the center circle. Why? As an expression of your intentionality. You are symbolically

It's Time To "Just Do It"

declaring that you are covenanting with God's purposes to become the Church that meets in your house (or dorm room, or office)! O.K., that was easy. So, let's move on to the next step.

Make a Prayer List - Next, in the box below begin writing in the names of people you want to pray for, asking God to bring them into your house church. Think creatively. These could include the names of friends, co-workers, neighbors, acquaintances, or people you know who are looking for a deeper and more meaningful walk with Christ. And, yes, they could even be those people at the secular coffee shop where you are playing chess and building relationships! Begin making these people the subjects of your focused prayers that God would bring them into the extended family of your organic house church.

Praying For Your "Multiplying House Church"

Use this space to make a list of people you want to pray for and invite to become part of your house church. Spend some time fasting and praying for them. Invite them to your initial potluck. As they respond positively, move their name from the list here to one of the circles above, until your Safe House of Hope And Prayer is full. Yes, It really can be that simple!

_____
_____
_____
_____
_____

River Houses Rising

I also know several house church planters who are focusing their prayers around Jesus' words in Luke 10:2, *"And He was saying to them, 'The harvest is plentiful, but the laborers are few; therefore beseech the Lord of the harvest to send out laborers into His harvest.'"* You can get started by praying over this verse, asking God to lead you to those people He wants to be part of the Church which meets in your house. Spend some time fasting and praying for the people on your list, or asking God to raise up people you don't even know yet; people He wants to be part of your house church. Fill your prayer list with people you are praying for.

Hold a Potluck - After a time of prayer and fasting for these people, invite them over for a gathering. Personally, we love potluck dinners. Why? **First**, it gives people a non-threatening way to get involved. Invite people to bring their favorite dish. My favorite saying is, *"If you feed them, they will come."* **Second**, people tend to relax over food and conversation around the table. My friend Wolfgang Simson calls these kinds of gatherings with food "meatings." They are more like family gatherings than religious meetings. Wolfgang likes to say that Jesus' ministry consisted of three things: He invited Himself over for dinner, told stories about the Kingdom of God, and healed people. The adventure of the Kingdom of God in organic house church is that Jesus wants to repeat His work in your house - or in their house!

At these initial gatherings you may do nothing more spiritual than talk about your spiritual desires, goals and aspirations. Ask people why they are there. Ask them to share - in five

It's Time To "Just Do It"

minutes or less - what they think God is doing in their lives. Listen to the questions people are asking and the issues they may be struggling with. Don't launch into giving religious answers to religious questions no one is asking. People don't want answers as much as they want to know they have the freedom to share without being condemned. Pray for one another's needs. Schedule a time for your next gathering, and call it a night. It really can be that simple.

Start Filling In Circles - As people begin to respond positively to the challenge of meeting together as a house church you can begin moving their names to one of the circles on your diagram (generally, one family or unmarried person per circle). Soon your house church diagram will be filled and you will have a visual illustration of what God is doing in your midst, not to mention a helpful aid for who to pray for (if you're like me, it helps to be able to see what you're praying for. My memory isn't what it once was and I need to be reminded!).

Teach Others To Do The Same - For those of you who don't like the idea of diagrams and circles (especially if you're recovering from a bad "network marketing" experience!) you need to understand that there are a couple of basic principles at work here. The first is a principle of *"simplicity and reproduction"* which basically says, *"Don't practice or model anything that cannot be reproduced and modeled by the majority of the people in your group."* Your goal should not be to impress others with how much you know (*"You need to sit and listen to my wonderful Bible teaching"*), but to teach

River Houses Rising

others how to become the church in their house by modeling things they can easily reproduce. Simple things are easier to model and easier to reproduce than complicated things. Conversely, the more complicated something is, the less likely it is to be modeled and reproduced.

And this leads to a second basic organic house church principle: *"Prepare and equip people to succeed in your absence."* As God blesses and your organic house church begins to function and grow, they day will come when either you or they will leave (hopefully to start other house churches). Prepare them for that day by teaching the same reproducible concepts to each participant so that they, too, can become "consciously intentional" about what it means to become a reproducing and multiplying house church. The more you make them dependent upon you (i.e., by giving them a complicated model that only you can do), the more you impart to them the DNA of a "spiritual mule" who will NEVER reproduce. They will NOT be able to succeed in your absence. You have condemned them to lives of spiritual dependency and immaturity. Is that what you want? Is that what Jesus wants for His Church?

Remember The Four Stages

If you have made it this far, I can only assume that you have made the decision to get started (otherwise, a wise man would have spared himself any further pain or irritation by abandoning this book!). We have discovered that people tend to go through four basic stages or phases on their

It's Time To "Just Do It"

journey into organic house church. By making a decision to actually get started you have, in fact, moved beyond **Stage #1** and have moved on into **Stage #2.** But let's quickly review all four stages.

⇨ **Stage #1 -** *The Dream Stage*. This is the stage at which people think to themselves, *"Wouldn't it be wonderful if . . .."* In other words, this is when people dream about what life in the Kingdom of God (including "church") could be like if only they were to follow the New Testament pattern as seen in such passages as Acts 2:41-47. Such dreaming often leads to **Stage #2.**

⇨ **Stage #2 -** *The Experimental Stage*. This is the stage when people decide to take the plunge and give it a try. It is usually during this experimental stage when people begin to discover that *"many are called, but few can stand it!"* If you persevere through the experimental stage (some people don't, because perseverance takes work and dedication), then you will eventually find yourself in **Stage #3.**

⇨ **Stage #3 -** *The Practitioner Stage*. At some point you will realize that you are no longer experimenting *with "this house church thing."* You have, in fact, become a 1 Corinthians 14-style house church and you are a genuine house church practitioner. You have become the organic church which meets in your house, and an authentic manifestation of the Kingdom of God.

⇨ **Stage #4 -** *The Teacher Stage*. It is a basic rule of life that

River Houses Rising

you can't teach what you don't do. Unless you are actually doing it your teaching simply won't ring true or authentic. In organic house church we teach by modeling. People who have become actual house church practitioners soon discover that, by their consistent example and model, they are teaching others how to become the church which meets in their house.

Reaching Beyond Your House Church
(And Into Your Neighborhood)

Before we leave the topic of how to get started, I want to share a few additional thoughts on being an organic house church which both meets in your home and which reaches out to your extended neighborhood. Remember that in our very mobile society your neighbors may include not only people who live down the street from you, but also people who are in your wider circle of influence. John Wesley, the great English evangelist and founder of the Methodist Church, liked to say, *"the world is my parish."* And that was in the day when people traveled by horse back and sailing ship. Today, your extended neighborhood may include everything within half-an-hour's driving distance and everyone you know and do business with in that sphere of influence: the kids' soccer coach, your daughter's dance instructor, the clerks at the supermarket, the staff at your favorite coffee shop and many more.

Get to Know Your Neighbors. Have you gotten to know these extended neighbors. Who are they? What are their

It's Time To "Just Do It"

names? What do they do for a living? What about their children? Do they have special needs or circumstances. The effective communication of the gospel often begins at the point of someone's need, crisis or "yearning." What is their religious background (if any!)? Do they go to church somewhere? When is their birthday? Why not invite them over for your next house church gathering or potluck. There is no reason why your neighbors should have to leave their neighborhood in order to have a genuine experience of the Kingdom of God! Why can't they experience the Kingdom of God in your living room (or, better yet, in theirs!)? Why should they need to go to a "healing room" when God can touch and heal them right there in your living room (or better yet, in theirs!)?

Pray for Your Neighbors and Your Neighborhood. Prayer really does make a difference. As Oswald Chambers once declared, *"Prayer doesn't prepare us for the greater work, prayer is the greater work."* Consistent, biblically-based prayer for others is the life-breath of the Kingdom of God. A strong prayer foundation is vital to the effectiveness of any organic house church, which is why we suggested that you make a prayer list earlier (See? There WAS a reason for that tacky diagram!). So, make your prayer list and set aside a regular day for prayer and fasting for your extended circle of friends and neighbors. You might even want to keep a prayer journal to record how God is answering your prayers.

Manifest the love of God . Preaching is easy. Living out a Jesus-shaped spirituality before a watching world is more

River Houses Rising

challenging. Our Postmodern culture is tired of hearing Christians preach one thing (such as the sanctity of marriage) and live out another (infidelity, spouse or child abuse, divorce, pornography, etc). Our message has been compromised by our lifestyles. Being a *Safe House of Hope And Prayer* means living an authentic lifestyle of genuinely caring for those around us. What good does it do to tell the world you love God with all your heart, soul, mind and strength if you aren't willing to love your neighbor as yourself (Matthew 22:37-38)?

Cultivate genuine non-judgmental friendships. It is a sad testimony that we Christians are frequently known for our negative attitudes. According to author David Kinnamen in his book, **UnChristian**, people outside of the Church regard Christians as being anti-gay (91%), judgmental (87%), and hypocritical (85%).[28] Unfortunately, such negative attitudes towards Christians are often well deserved. Let's face reality. Many Christians struggle with personal judgmentalism toward the "messiness" of other people's lives. But Jesus had no such struggle. And if Jesus could be comfortable hanging out with *"tax collectors and sinners"* (Matthew 9:10) without condemning them, why can't we? It is not our calling to play the Holy Spirit or to judge others and impose our external religious legalism (*"You mustn't dance, drink, smoke or chew or run around with girls who do"*). Religious legalism and

---

[28] David Kinneman and Dave Lyons, **unChristian: What a New Generation Really Thinks about Christianity and Why It Matters** (Grand Rapids: Baker Books, 2007).

It's Time To "Just Do It"

judgmentalism will destroy your ministry and will spread a false DNA which teaches people that Christian spirituality and the Kingdom of God can be reduced to a set of religious rules. God has not called us to be judges. That's His job. We've been called to befriend the marginalized and bear witnesses to the transforming power of the Kingdom of God.

Become a listener. People need to know that you care about what is important to them. Listen to them talk about the struggles or challenges in their lives without judging them, criticizing them or preaching at them. Then, make the issues of their lives the objects of your specific prayers.

Build relationships. Celebrate birthdays, anniversaries and other significant life-events. When a drug dealer who had come into our ministry had to go to prison on an old charge, we threw a "going to jail party" at his apartment and then walked him over to the jail where he turned himself in. At his sentencing hearing earlier that day I had asked the judge to release him into my custody on my assurance that I would see that he turned himself in at 5PM that evening. Much to the surprise and irritation of the Prosecutor, the Judge agreed and we had a house church party to send him off to jail! The result was a neighborhood house church in his apartment!

River Houses Rising

Questions For Reflection

Reflecting on this Chapter, what did you learn about being an organic house church that you did not know before?

When it comes to organic house church, what is preventing you from *"Just Doing It"*?

What specific steps are you taking to express your own intentionality when it comes to making disciples?

What specific steps have you taken to begin reaching out to people outside of your comfortable circle of Christian friends?

Safe Houses of Hope And Prayer offers a simple and reproducible concept of organic house church that you can easily start, easily model and easily reproduce in the lives of those around you. Remember our motto: *"Just Do It!"*

Chapter 10

A Time To Dance

In the previous chapter we talked about some of the practical steps to get started doing organic house church. Those steps are good and necessary. But in this chapter I want to talk just a little about what it means to function as an organic house church. And for this organic house church lesson I'm going to look for help from Fred Astaire.

Old Movies, Fred Astaire And House Church

I confess I love old movies. I'm one of those afficionados who genuinely believes that the best overall movie ever made was (and still is) *"Casablanca"* with Humphrey Bogart, Ingred Bergman and a cast of outstanding classic actors. And, yes, I even have the 50th Year Anniversary Edition, just in case you were wondering (which you probably weren't).

When my wife and I are in the mood for a good movie, we often turn to an old classic. And nothing is more classic than watching an old song and dance musical like *"The Band Wagon"* (1953). There Fred Astaire dances with Cyd Charisse to the music of *"Dancing In The Dark"* (music by Arthur Schwartz and lyrics by Howard Dietz). Talk about beautiful music combined with incredible gracefulness. It's the story of two very different people who must learn to dance together, despite their differences (sound familiar?).

River Houses Rising

And if you think that's tough, in *"Royal Wedding"* Fred Astaire dances with a hat rack, making the hat rack look good and the whole thing look easy!

So, what's all this got to do with organic house church, you ask? Well, as my daughter says when we're translating Greek together, *"Wait for it, dad, wait for it!"*

If you ask the question *"What is house church?"* among house church participants you'll get a wide variety of answers, which reflect the varying interests, experiences and emphasis of the different house churches. If you were to visit on one particular evening devoted to prayer and worship, you might conclude (both rightly and wrongly) that house church was a prayer meeting. If you were to visit on a different night when teaching was being emphasized you might conclude (again, rightly and wrongly) that house church is all about teaching. On yet another night when a mature 5-fold prophetic individual is ministering you might conclude that house church is all about giving and receiving prophetic words. And on still another night when God is moving and all the gifts are functioning through many people you might conclude that house church is borderline pandemonium. And, again, you would be both right and wrong.

By now you should be getting the point. Organic house church is about ALL of these things, and yet, it is about NONE of these things. So, allow me to return now to my dancing metaphor (Admit it. The suspense of how I was going to tie all this together was killing you!). House church,

A Time To Dance

like our individual relationships with God, is about learning to dance with God . . . and then with one another. Dancing represents a very intimate relationship between two people. It requires communication, practice, allowing someone else to lead (giving up control!) while you and I follow, and becoming so intimately acquainted with another person that you can sense (and eventually anticipate) their every move by looking in their eye, listening to the tone of their voice or feeling the inflection of their body. And it requires a deep level of trust.

If you have ever watched ice dancers in the Olympic Games, then you have seen the intricate moves which require each partner to trust one another, often at substantial personal risk. But when it comes together it is beautiful to watch. I still vividly remember Jayne Torvill and Christopher Dean performing their intricate and intimate ice dancing program to Ravel's *"Bolero"* at the 1984 Winter Olympics in Sarajevo, earning them 12 perfect 6.0s and a gold medal. It was . . . unforgettable!

A Time To Dance

O.K., let's go back to the question: *"What is organic house church?"* At its most basic and intimate level, organic house church is the pursuit of God in the company of friends who are learning to dance . . . with God and with one another. Is house church about more than that. Yes, of course it is. It's about revival, good teaching, prayer, good deeds, church planting, discipling the nations and much more. But

River Houses Rising

ultimately, all of those "other things" are dependent for their success upon believers who are willing to discover, practice and learn the intricate and intimate art of dancing with God and with one another.

Several years ago blind Christian recording artist Ken Medema recorded a song entitled *"She Asked Me to Dance"* that I'll never forget. I have since lost the album (O.K., bigger than a CD and played on something called a record player - just in case you were wondering), but the words went like this:

> *He asked me to dance*
> *though I'd never tried dancing before,*
> *I had visions of saints and angels*
> *laughing us right off the floor.*
> *Although I protested it just wouldn't be any good,*
> *He gently insisted and finally I told him I would.*
> *Unforgettable, he was the coming of Spring*
> *on a cold winter's day;*
> *Unforgettable, he taught this singer to sing*
> *in a whole new way.*

So, tell me. How are your dancing skills coming along, both with God and with the other believers in your house church? This is a challenge for those of us who have grown up and spent most of our Christian lives in traditional institutional churches where what little "dancing" that occurred was very carefully scripted and choreographed to make everyone (particularly the professional staff) look good. Unfortunately

A Time To Dance

many people want to bring this carefully rehearsed script into organic house church, and the results are nearly always disappointing.

As the coming season of awakening and spiritual outpouring begins, I believe God is once again going to teach His people the intimate and intricate art of dancing with Him and with one another. There is a certain degree of risk here, the risk of *"saints and angels laughing us right off the floor."* But trust me (and I'm still learning this). If Fred Astaire can dance with a hat rack and make it look good, even easy, chances are that Jesus can dance with you and your house church, and make it . . . *unforgettable!*

Questions For Reflection

Reflecting on this Chapter, explain how practicing organic house church is like learning to dance with someone you've never met or danced with before? How is it different?

Safe Houses of Hope And Prayer is an organic house church gathering in your house where believers are learning the intimate and intricate art of dancing with God and with one another.

River Houses Rising

Chapter 11

Discovering People Of Peace

"After this the Lord appointed seventy-two others and sent them on ahead of him, two by two, into every town and place where he himself was about to go. And he said to them, 'The harvest is plentiful, but the laborers are few. Therefore pray earnestly to the Lord of the harvest to send out laborers into his harvest. Go your way; behold, I am sending you out as lambs in the midst of wolves. Carry no moneybag, no knapsack, no sandals, and greet no one on the road. Whatever house you enter, first say, 'Peace be to this house!' And if a son of peace is there, your peace will rest upon him. But if not, it will return to you. And remain in the same house, eating and drinking what they provide, for the laborer deserves his wages.'" (Luke 10:1-7)

Are You A Person of Peace?

Several years ago I attended a conference about organic house church. One of the leadership team for the conference was an individual from Germany named Bruno. He and I had some good conversations over the course of the weekend, but I will never forget one comment he made, *"We don't plant house churches with Christians,"* he said in his gruff German accent, *"Too much baggage."* Now, several years later, I know exactly what Bruno meant.

River Houses Rising

All too often, Christians are NOT people of peace. Not really. A lot of times we aren't even likeable. We tend to be overly opinionated and talk when we should be listening. We give answers to questions people aren't really asking (but which seem to be very important to US). We argue points of theology or doctrine that interest no one but us. We insist that our particular way of prayer, Bible study, worship, music, etc. is the right and biblical way that everyone should follow. We are so convinced that Jesus supports our particular political views that outsiders think they must endorse our political beliefs or join our political party (conservative or liberal) in order to participate in our church. We are quick to judge the "messiness" of other people's lives and pronounce them sinful while failing to recognize or confront our own issues (hmm, didn't Jesus say something about a log in your eye - Matthew 7:3).

As I shared in the previous chapter, author David Kinnamen discovered that people outside of the Church regard Christians as being anti-gay (91%), judgmental (87%), and hypocritical (85%). They're pretty sure we don't love God as much as we claim to, and they're convinced that we don't love them as much as we love ourselves. And the list goes on. And then we wonder why our unbelieving friends and neighbors don't want to go to church with us. Quite frankly, why should they?! And unless we change these bad behaviors they won't want to come to our house church either. Why should they? What's changed? Are we *really* people of peace?

Discovering People Of Peace

People of Peace

Let's go back to the passage from the gospel of Luke which we saw at the opening of this chapter. What we have in that passage from Luke Chapter 10 is a snap shot of how Jesus instructed His followers to "do evangelism." The early New Testament church didn't "do evangelism" as you and I understand it. They proclaimed the Kingdom, they taught the Kingdom and they lived the Kingdom, and people responded to what they SAW and HEARD. And when it came to spreading the message of the Kingdom, Jesus taught his disciples to look for key players He described as "people of peace."[29]

So, what exactly is a "person of peace"? From what we can glean from Scripture this is a person sovereignly prepared by God to receive the good news about the Kingdom. How can we identify them? Let me suggest three possible characteristics that we can look for.

Receptivity. A person of peace could be someone who is already interested in and open to the gospel, to the Kingdom of God and to the possibility of God working in their lives. Our traditional mentality has always been that we must first sow,

---

[29]The companion passage to this one in Luke is found in Matthew Chapter 10 where Jesus instructs His disciples on how they should conduct themselves when they go out in His name. In Luke 10 Jesus repeats these instructions only this time He is instructing the 72, instead of the 12. In Luke 10 Jesus instructs the 72 in what it means to be and to find a Person of Peace.

River Houses Rising

sow, sow, and then we can harvest. But what if God has already done the preparation and sowing? This seems to be what Jesus is saying in John 4:35-38.

"Do you not say, 'There are yet four months, then comes the harvest'? Look, I tell you, lift up your eyes, and see that the fields are white for harvest. Already the one who reaps is receiving wages and gathering fruit for eternal life, so that sower and reaper may rejoice together. For here the saying holds true, 'One sows and another reaps.' I sent you to reap that for which you did not labor. Others have labored, and you have entered into their labor." (John 4:35-38)

Sometimes God has already done the sowing before we ever arrive, and He has sovereignly brought us to this person of peace in order to finish what He has already started. We have the privilege of reaping where God has already sown. This is the principle we see at work here in Luke 10. Jesus teaches and demonstrates that by finding a person of peace, we can reap where God has already sown. After they have responded positively to the Gospel we may have the opportunity to sow effectively into the <u>oikos</u> (that's the Greek word for our extended family or household) of that person!

Scripture illustrates this principle with several examples, but we'll just highlight three: 1) the conversion of Cornelius in Acts 10, 2) the conversion of Lydia in Acts 16:14, and 3) the conversion of the Philippian Jailer in Acts 16:30. These three events illustrate that you can harvest first by finding a receptive "person of peace." Once they respond, then you

Discovering People Of Peace

can begin sowing within their household and beyond. It is all of God. God has, in fact, gone before you to prepare these hearts!

Reputation. A person of peace can be a person of a known reputation, and that reputation can be either good or bad. For example, in Mark Chapter 5 Jesus lands at Gadara and is greeted by a demoniac who is violent, naked, in broken chains, and has a ***horrible*** reputation. Everyone in the area is afraid of him! BUT God has sovereignly placed him there, desperate and ready for an encounter with Jesus! He is not the kind of person that you and I would normally see as a strong candidate to be a "person of peace," but that is exactly what he became! After he had been delivered from his demonic affliction, this man begged Jesus for permission to go with Him. But Jesus sent him back to Decapolis (his neighborhood) to tell his story to his family and friends, that is, to sow back into his own *oikos* (i.e., extended family). Do you think he had a powerful story to tell? In fact, it was so powerful that when Jesus returned to that area in Mark 7:31-37, we read that the residents of that area came to Him with their needs, *"they brought to Him one who was deaf and spoke with difficulty, and they entreated Him to lay His hand upon him."* The demoniac's family and friends had seen a changed man and the entire region responded by bringing more people to Jesus. The former demoniac had become a Godly "man of peace," proclaiming Jesus and witnessing to the power of the Kingdom of God. The story of the Gadarene demoniac is a wonderful example of how Jesus can raise up a notorious person of peace, and by transforming their life He

River Houses Rising

can sow kingdom seed into the lives of many more.

Another example of this principle can be seen in the life of the woman of Samaria in John Chapter 4. She was a person with a well-known reputation (notorious might be a more apt description) in her village. But after her conversion her reputation and notoriety enabled her to bring the entire village to Jesus.

Hospitality. A person of peace can be a person of unexpected hospitality. Zaccheus was such a person. In Luke Chapter 9 Jesus is passing through the town of Jericho when he encounters Zaccheus, a man with a notorious reputation. He was universally despised because he was the chief tax collector for that area. Jesus showed Zaccheus kindness by asking to come to his house. Zaccheus could have declined, but instead he showed hospitality by gladly receiving Jesus. The result was two-fold. The first result was a very irritated religious leadership who regarded Zaccheus as "a sinner" and who condemned Jesus for associating with him. The second result was a transforming encounter between Jesus and Zaccheus that undoubtedly had profound ripple effects throughout Jericho.

Cornelius: A Soldier and Man of Peace

One of the best biblical examples of this principle at work can be seen in the story of Cornelius in Acts Chapter 10. Cornelius (we don't know his full name) lived in Roman occupied Palestine in the 1st Century A.D. The story we have

Discovering People Of Peace

about him comes from around A.D. 45. He was a Roman military officer (a Centurion) assigned to a Roman Legion headquartered in the strategic town of Caesarea, on the northwest coast of Palestine. From all accounts he appears to have been an honorable man with good standing in the community. He had even befriended the local Jewish community and had shown interest in their religion. The Jewish community in turn had honored him by calling him a "god-fearer" (a high compliment) and his spiritual interest appeared genuine. Then something happened to this praying, god-fearing Roman that changed the course of his life.

One day, while Cornelius was praying, an angel appeared to him and informed him that God had heard his prayers. The angel told Cornelius to send for a man named Simon who was staying in the coastal town of Joppa, about one day's travel away. Bewildered (and afraid) but obedient, Cornelius sent two servants and a soldier to Joppa to find this man named Simon. While God was doing all of this in Cornelius' life, God was also sovereignly preparing Simon for what was about to happen, but that's a separate story. When Simon arrived at the house of Cornelius three days later he found that this god-fearing "man of peace" was not alone. Cornelius had invited all of his relatives and close friends in Caesarea to come and hear what this man Simon was going to say. It must be important, since an angel had arranged the whole thing! Cornelius introduced himself to Simon, explained to him all that had happened and said, *"We are all here present in the sight of God, to hear all that you have been*

River Houses Rising

commanded by the Lord."

What a moment for both Cornelius and for Simon, both realizing that they were each part of a divinely orchestrated moment much bigger than themselves! Realizing that God had gone before him to prepare this "man of peace," Simon, also named Peter, knew God was about to do something wonderful in the life of this god-fearing man of peace. *"Truly I understand that God shows no partiality,"* Simon began, *"but in every nation anyone who fears him and does what is right is acceptable to him."* The words began to flow now as Simon remembered and described the events that had forever changed his life. *"As for the word that he sent to Israel, preaching good news of peace through Jesus Christ (he is Lord of all), you yourselves know what happened throughout all Judea, beginning from Galilee after the baptism that John proclaimed: how God anointed Jesus of Nazareth with the Holy Spirit and with power. He went about doing good and healing all who were oppressed by the devil, for God was with him. And we are witnesses of all that he did both in the country of the Jews and in Jerusalem. They put him to death by hanging him on a tree, but God raised him on the third day and made him to appear, not to all the people but to us who had been chosen by God as witnesses, who ate and drank with him after he rose from the dead. And he commanded us to preach to the people and to testify that he is the one appointed by God to be judge of the living and the dead. To him all the prophets bear witness that everyone who believes in him receives forgiveness of sins through his name."* (Acts 10:34-43)

Discovering People Of Peace

Then it happened. Simon was still speaking when the presence and power of God filled the room, touching Cornelius, his entire family and everyone present. And Peter, the former man of peace and fisherman from Galilee, watched in amazement as the sovereign God answered the cry of another searching heart and swept another "person of peace" into the peaceable Kingdom of God.

Which Are You?

So, let me ask you two questions. **First**, are you a person of peace, or are you among the too-much-baggage believers Bruno referred to, or the anti-gay, judgmental, and hypocritical Christians many non-Christians see in the Church? There is a spiritual principle I can't explain but which I have seen far too often to deny, and it is this: *"Like attracts like."* If you are a baggage-laden angry, contentious, judgmental, hypocritical religionist in pursuit of a religion-shaped spirituality that you call "church," that is the kind of person you will attract, and the kind of people you will be attracted to. Like attracts like. But if you are a genuine Kingdom-minded believer in pursuit of a Jesus-shaped spirituality - a genuine person of peace in your own *oikos* (extended family) - then those are the kind of people you will attract and the kind of people you will be attracted to.

Second, are you on the look-out for other people of peace who may be receptive to what God wants to do? They may take the form of a neighbor who asks you for a favor (*"Could you watch our house while we're gone for the weekend"*) or

River Houses Rising

who invites you over for dinner. It could take the form of a co-worker who invites you out for drinks or an after work party. That may be their way of showing hospitality and inviting you into their circle of influence to meet their friends. Personally, I think Jesus would have accepted the invitation. Will you? Being a *Safe House of Hope And Prayer* means being a person of peace in our sphere of influence and then asking God to lead us to other people of peace whom God has already prepared with a hunger for the Kingdom of God.

Questions For Reflection

Reflecting on this Chapter, what did you learn about the idea of a "person of peace" that you did not know before?

Can you identify other "persons of peace" in the New Testament? How did God use them?

Reflecting on this Chapter and your own personal experience, can you think of a "person of peace" you have known who had a significant impact for the Kingdom?

Safe Houses of Hope And Prayer represents people of peace looking to connect with other people of peace in their extended sphere of influence in order to have an impact for the Kingdom of God.

Chapter 12

Contagious DNA

The year was approximately A.D. 117. In the city of Smyrna in the Roman Province of Asia (modern day western Turkey) a persecution of Christians had broken out. The newly arrived Roman Governor, Pliny the Elder, was an accomplished Roman jurist. But Pliny had never encountered Christians before and was unsure how to proceed with placing them on trial, so he wrote to his friend, the Emperor Trajan, asking for instructions. In the course of his correspondence Pliny makes the following observation:

*"I therefore postponed the investigation and hastened to consult you. For the matter seemed to me to warrant consulting you, especially because of the number involved. For many persons of every age, every rank, and also of both sexes are and will be endangered. For **the contagion** of this superstition has spread not only to the cities but also to the villages and farms."*

Did you catch what he said? From Pliny's perspective as an outside observer, the faith of those early believers was spreading like a *"contagion"* through cities, villages and farms. Those early believers were infected with a spiritual DNA that was viral and highly contagious.

Genuine biblical faith, manifesting the Kingdom of God and

River Houses Rising

lived out by individuals in pursuit of a Jesus-shaped spirituality, has always been contagious. Author and missiologist Alan Hirsch describes the faith of those early believers as "sneezable," summed up by the simple declaration, *"Jesus is Lord."* It was a message simple enough to "sneeze" and contagious enough to spread. The goal of organic house church and *Safe Houses of Hope And Prayer* is to recapture that viral DNA which makes Christianity a "sneezable" and contagious faith.

The DNA of the Coming Move of God

At the risk of boring some of you , we should start with a definition of DNA from our friends at Wikipedia:

"Deoxyribonucleic acid, or DNA is a nucleic acid molecule that contains the genetic instructions used in the development and functioning of all living organisms. The main role of DNA is the long-term storage of information and it is often compared to a set of blueprints, since DNA contains the instructions needed to construct other components of cells, such as proteins and RNA molecules."

O.K., here's the point. Organic house church is a living organism. It has a spiritual DNA - a spiritual blueprint - for reproduction and growth that will determine what the end product of that reproduction looks like and how quickly it will spread. Good DNA produces good outcomes. Bad DNA produces bad outcomes. The lesson is simple: What is the spiritual DNA of your organic house church and what is it

Contagious DNA

producing that is worth multiplying? I believe God has a specific DNA for the coming move of His Spirit through organic house churches, and that's where I want to turn our attention now.

During the Great Welsh Revival of 1904 Evan Roberts declared, *"Bend the Church, Save the world."* Apparently, saving the world is easy. Bending the Church is hard. God "bent" Evan Roberts in September of 1904 and the world felt the impact of one "bent" life. A few years ago several members of our house church network had an encounter with God which "bent" us profoundly, and transformed our understanding of what God wants to do in and through organic house churches in this coming move of His Spirit. It established in us what we believe will prove to be the spiritual DNA of this coming outpouring of God's Spirit.[30] And I want to share it with you now.

The big lesson which I took away from that profound "bending" experience with God was this: We are entering a profound season of divine visitation and spiritual outpouring during which the River of God's Spirit is going to flow with great power and blessing through organic house churches. And at the very outset God is seeking to sow a basic spiritual DNA into this unfolding move of His Spirit. This DNA consists of three specific characteristics or DNA markers. Here they

---

[30]You can read my account of this encounter in *"Chapter 4 - What The Angels Said"* of our book, ***The Inextinguishable Blaze: God's Call to Holiness, Repentance, Intimacy And Spiritual Awakening***, available on our website from Amazon.com.

River Houses Rising

are: 1) Holiness and the fear of the Lord, 2) Repentance, and 3) Intimacy. When the Holy Spirit breathes these three things into your life and the life of your organic house church they will make you "contagious" beyond your wildest expectations. That's why I want to spend some time explaining each of these.

DNA Marker # 1: Holiness And The Fear Of God

"Since we have these promises, beloved, let us cleanse ourselves from every defilement of body and spirit, bringing holiness to completion in the fear of God." (2 Corinthians 7:1)

We need to take a moment and define "holiness." Here goes: *"Holiness is that attribute of God's nature whereby He is totally and completely separated from sin and is singularly devoted to His own glory."*

Stephen Charnock, the 17th century English Puritan divine, summed up God's holiness when he observed, *"Power is God's hand or arm, omniscience His eye, mercy His bowels, eternity His duration, but holiness is His beauty."*

For the believer who shares the divine nature (2 Peter 1:4) and is commanded to *." . . be holy, for I am holy"* (1 Peter 1:16), holiness exists in two parts. On the one hand, holiness has to do with our separation and purity from sin. On the other hand, holiness has to do with our being devoted to serving and pursuing God's glory.

Contagious DNA

But holiness is not the product of human effort. Like the glow which shone from Moses' face after meeting with God (Exodus 34:29ff), holiness is the result of a genuine encounter with God. Holiness isn't legalism, and legalism is not holiness. Legalism and rules (*"I don't drink, dance, smoke or chew, or run around with girls who do"*) are like the veil which Moses continued to wear over His face (2 Corinthians 3:13) so people would not know that the glow of God's presence was fading. Without the Presence of God, holiness fades away and devolves into religious rules - legalism masquerading as holiness. Genuine holiness is us manifesting the very nature of the God Who is holy and Who invites us to the same through repentance and greater intimacy with Himself. And no set of rules can ever produce that. It is the product of a genuine visitation from God.

Because we do not appreciate the holiness of God, we do not fear Him in any genuine biblical sense. The people of Israel discovered both the holiness and the fear of God when they stood before God at the foot of Mount Horeb in Exodus 19. Isaiah rudely discovered this fear when he was confronted in the Temple by a vision of God in all His terrible holiness (Isaiah 6:ff). That encounter with God's holiness transformed Isaiah. And Isaiah discovered what David meant when he wrote under the inspiration of the Holy Spirit, *"The fear of the Lord is clean . . ."* (Psalm 19:9). The New Testament Church was rudely introduced to God's holiness when He struck Ananias and Sapphira dead where they stood for the sin of intentionally lying to the Holy Spirit (see Acts Chapter 5) . The impact of that encounter with God's holiness upon both the Church and the larger community was profound: *"And great fear came upon the whole church, and upon all who heard of these things"* (Acts 5:11). God's holiness is not something to be trifled with.

In the coming spiritual outpouring, God Himself intends to visit His Church and to mark His Church with the DNA of His holiness with the result of returning *"the fear of the Lord"* to His people. How is He going to do this? I don't know. That's why He is God and I'm not! What I do know is that the history of great spiritual outpourings makes it clear that God is able. And when the holiness and fire of God's presence ignites in His church in the genuine *"fear of the Lord,"* it will become both a spreading wildfire and a spreading "sneezable" contagion once again.

DNA Trait # 2: Repentance

"If the foundations are destroyed, what shall the righteous do?" Psalm 11:3

The ancient Hebrew Psalmist (David) understood something which we have forgotten, namely, that certain things are foundational. A truth is foundational if its removal jeopardizes whatever you are seeking to build. In the Church of God, repentance is a foundational truth. Remove it, and the very nature and existence of the Church is threatened. Exactly how foundational is repentance to the biblical message? That's easy. It *IS* the biblical message. Don't take my word for it. Listen to the words of Jesus (and John the Baptist):

Contagious DNA

*"**Repent**, for the kingdom of heaven is at hand."*
(Matthew 3:2; 4:17; Mark 1:14-15).

One of the unsettling things about Jesus' message of repentance is that He directed it at the religion-shaped spirituality of His day, the very people whom the Old Testament Scriptures named as God's chosen people. If God's chosen people in Jesus' day were in need of repentance and a return to a Jesus-shaped spirituality, what besides our pride makes us think that His people today are somehow exempt from that same message?

Unfortunately, repentance has become the "lost heart" of God's people today. One seldom hears messages on the need for personal or corporate repentance from sin. And yet when we look at the New testament there are some 58 references to the need to repent. "Repent" is the most frequent instruction given by the risen Christ to the 7 Churches of Asia in Revelation Chapters 2 and 3 (occurring 6 times).[31] Repentance is a matter close to God's heart.

Many Christians make the mistake of thinking that repentance is only about repenting of sin. While this is an important reason and occasion for repentance, it is NOT the only reason and occasion for repentance. For example, repentance is one of the dominant themes of the book of

---

[31]See our book, ***When Jesus Visits His Church: A Study Of The Seven Churches of Asia (Revelation Chapters 2-3)***, available on our website from Amazon.com.

River Houses Rising

Jeremiah, God calling His people to repent of their sin, rebellion and spiritual adultery and return to Him. But in Chapter 15 God tells Jeremiah,

"Therefore thus says the LORD: 'If you return, I will restore you, and you shall stand before me. If you utter what is precious, and not what is worthless, you shall be as my mouth. They shall turn to you, but you shall not turn to them." (Jeremiah 15:19)

The word "return" in this verse is Jeremiah's regular word for "repent." But here the emphasis is not upon turning from sin, but turning away from other things that distract from focusing upon God and His will. God is telling Jeremiah that if he will turn his focus away from what is happening around him and turn towards the Lord as his sole focus, then God will restore Jeremiah (literally, *"I will turn to you"*) and cause Jeremiah to stand before Him as His spokes person. In essence, God is telling Jeremiah that repentance on his part will result in greater intimacy with God. Think of it as Jeremiah turning to God and God responding by turning to Jeremiah, with the result that both get more intimate "face time" together.

In the coming season of spiritual outpouring God is seeking a repentant people. He wants a people whose first impulse is to repent by turning their focus away from anything and everything that distracts from holiness and intimacy with God and to focus their attention solely upon Him.

Now, what does this mean for your house church? Simple.

Contagious DNA

Are the people in your house church still focused upon murmuring about the failings of the traditional or institutional church? Then it's time to repent, and to get your focus upon the God Whose church it is in spite of its many failings. It's time to focus upon what God has called you to be and do, not upon what He has called you to leave. Are people in your house church still carrying around the wounds of past church experiences? Then it is time to repent, and to stop focusing upon your woundedness and to begin focusing upon the LORD our healer Who heals the broken hearted (Psalm 147:3). Are you starting to get the picture here? Repentance is not *just* about repenting from sin. It is also about getting our focus off of those things which distract us from the Lord and intimacy with Him. It is about restoring the Lord and *"the beauty of His holiness"* as our focus. Is a spirit of repentance part of the DNA of your house church? If not, now would be a good time to start by asking God to restore such a spirit in your midst.

DNA Trait # 3: Intimacy

"When Thou didst say, 'Seek My face,' my heart said to Thee, 'Thy face, O Lord, I shall seek'" (Psalm 27:8, NASB)

Let me shake and bend your paradigm a little with this statement: You cannot have genuine intimacy with God without genuine repentance from those things which distract your focus from Him. Genuine repentance is the doorway to greater intimacy with God. We see this reflected in Psalm 24 when the Psalmist says,

River Houses Rising

"Who shall ascend the hill of the LORD? And who shall stand in his holy place? He who has clean hands and a pure heart, who does not lift up his soul to what is false and does not swear deceitfully." (Psalm 24:3-4, NASB)

To stand in God's holy place is to have intimate fellowship with him, but to get there one must have *"clean hands and a pure heart."* How do we get clean hands and a pure heart? Through repentance, the confession of sin and the turning away from those things which fill our hearts and hands with "other things" (rather than "the main thing") and turn our focus away from Him.

When the Church at Ephesus in Revelation 2:4 left their first love and lost their intimacy with Jesus, the answer to restoring that love and that intimacy wasn't better worship music or even a better sermon. Rather, it was repentance. When the tepid believers of Laodicea discovered Jesus on the outside of their church seeking entrance (wow, talk about lost intimacy!), the answer to restored intimacy was simple: ." . . be zealous, therefore, and repent." (Revelation 3:19-20).[32]

Much of what passes for intimacy in the church today is "cheap intimacy," because it represents intimacy without repentance. Cheap intimacy is like cheap worship, an

---

[32]Again, for more on this see our book, ***When Jesus Visits His Church: A Study Of The Seven Churches of Asia (Revelation Chapters 2-3)***, available on our website from Amazon.com.

Contagious DNA

emotionally stimulating experience which costs us little or nothing. No self-examination, no death to self, no repentance from sin or distractions, no discernment. Just more words, more music . . . and more distractions.

Is genuine intimacy with God part of the DNA of your house church? Genuine intimacy requires significant amounts of devoted "face time" between us and God. Are you as a house church pursuing genuine intimacy with God by spending a significant amount of time with God as a group - praying, worshiping, waiting in silence, and, yes, repenting before the Lord? In this coming move of God's Spirit it is God Himself who wants to restore genuine intimacy between Himself and His Church. Our role is to seek Him in repentant expectation. He will do the rest.

You Can't Teach Your Way To Better DNA

I hope this doesn't come to you as a shock, but most traditional Churches in America are led by teachers, not pastors (yes, even if the sign on his office door says "Pastor"). Being the good rationalists that we are, we genuinely believe that the key to right thinking and behavior is good teaching. So, the battle cry of the "pastor search committee" of the average church is something like this, *"We need someone who is an excellent Bible teacher."* And that is, indeed, what they usually get. A teacher.

Now, don't get me wrong. Teaching is a valuable and worthy gift in the Church. But the blind spot of a teacher is the belief

River Houses Rising

that all problems in the life of the individual and the church can be solved with better teaching. A gifted teacher has never met a problem that he (or she) couldn't teach his way out of. Are people in your church having marital problems? Bring in the teachers to teach on biblical marriage. Is giving down and stewardship a problem? Bring in the financial management teachers to teach biblical financial principles. But marriages continue to fail at an alarming and growing rate, and Christian giving as a percentage of income continues to fall (down 35% in 35 years). Why? Because as valuable as good teaching is, you cannot teach your way to better DNA! Good Bible teaching is the ordinary work of the Church, a task given to and performed by gifted 5-Fold teachers as part of the normal life of the Church. But changing the DNA of the Church represents the extra-ordinary work of the Holy Spirit.

O.K., you say, *"If you can't teach your way to better DNA, why are you teaching us about this?!"* Good question, grasshopper. And when you can take the pebble from my hand, it will be time for you to start your own house church (Oooops, sorry, old Kung Fu rerun just kicked in, again!). I am "teaching" you this so you will understand what God is about to do in and through His church. And if this is what God is about to do, you and I have an opportunity to actively pursue it (for example, through prayer and fasting) and to willingly participate. The rest is up to Him.

Contagious DNA

Conclusion

God is about to visit His Church and indelibly imprint new (but old) DNA upon her character (holiness and the fear of God, repentance and intimacy). Why? So that in the House Church generations yet to be born we will multiply and reproduce believers and churches where repentance, intimacy and holiness are the norm, just as the prophet Zechariah foresaw:

"And on that day there shall be inscribed on the bells of the horses, 'Holy to the LORD.' And the pots in the house of the LORD shall be as the bowls before the altar. And every pot in Jerusalem and Judah shall be holy to the LORD of hosts, so that all who sacrifice may come and take of them and boil the meat of the sacrifice in them." (Zechariah 14:20-21)

Questions For Reflection

Reflecting on this Chapter, what did you learn about God's plan for the DNA of organic house church?

How would you describe the DNA of your current church experience? How does it compare with what you learned in this Chapter?

Safe Houses of Hope And Prayer represents an organic house church in your house seeking God for the Spirit breathed DNA of holiness and the fear of God, genuine personal repentance and genuine intimacy with Him.

River Houses Rising

Chapter 13

God Has A Math Problem
(And You Can Help!)

The Church in America and Europe today is facing two dilemmas that are in reality one-and-the-same. The dilemma is both structural and mathematical. Here it is: The traditional Church as most of us have known it is built upon a structure that makes it ***physically and mathematically impossible*** to ever fulfill Christ's command to disciple the nations. Why? Because it is a structure that regards evangelism and the expansion of the Kingdom as a matter of simple addition. It isn't. And it never has been.

The Math of Revival And Megachurches

This is a bold declaration (in fact, a heretical declaration) that demands some explanation. So, let's illustrate this structural problem by examining the history of revivals and spiritual awakenings. According to revival historian Frank Grenville Beardsley, during the Great Awakening of Colonial America (1740s), *"more than 7% of the entire population of (the) colonies would have been gathered into the churches as a direct result of the revival."*[33] Similar figures are reported again by historian Byrnmor P. Jones who confirms that

---

[33] Frank Grenville Beardsley, ***A History of American Revivals***, 3rd Edition (American Tract Society: New York, 1912), p. 65

River Houses Rising

during the great Welsh Revival of 1904 some 5% of the population of Wales was converted and added to the church.[34] To summarize, the great revivals of the past have, on average, seen between five and seven percent (5-to-7%) of the larger population come to faith in Christ and join the Church. In an America of 300 million people, if the coming spiritual awakening produces only the historic average of new believers, this would mean a harvest of some 15-to-21 million new believers. Where are all of those new believers going to go for fellowship and discipleship? To the local megachurch? I think not.

Let's focus on that lower number of 15 million potential new believers. According to a database kept by *The Hartford Institute For Religion Research* there are 1,398 megachurches in America with a total average attendance of 5,154,758 people, or an average attendance of 3,687 people per church.[35] Based upon these average megachurch attendance numbers, in order to accommodate a wave of 15 million new believers you would need to build ***4,068 NEW megachurches***, and at what cost in time and resources? As I shared earlier in this book, my friend Jerry Twombly has spent his professional career helping churches raise money for building such churches. Jerry is now telling his clientele that the age of the megachurch is over. It is no longer a

---

[34]Brynmor P. Jones, ***Voices From The Welsh Revival 1904-1905*** (Evangelical Press of Wales: Bridgend, 1995), page 65-66.

[35]The Hartford Institute For Religion Research online at http://hirr.hartsem.edu/megachurch/database.html

God Has A Math Problem

financially viable model (if it ever was!). So, tripling the number of megachurches is financially out of the question. Besides, wouldn't it be better to invest that time and those resources in people rather than buildings, facilities, staff and programs?

I believe God has a different plan than tripling the number of megachurches on the religious landscape. I think God's plan is to raise up a new wineskin for the new wine of this coming harvest. That new wineskin is tens of thousands of organic, multiplying house churches where the focus is upon genuine worship, personal discipleship, biblical community and local outreach. Let's do some New Testament math to understand why.

A First Century Math Lesson

This problem of people and numbers first occurred in the Book of Acts in the ministry of the early Church. So that is where we want to begin our search for a solution to this problem. The early New Testament Church began its existence by experiencing phenomenal growth-by-addition. Three times in the Book of Acts (Acts 2:41; 2:47; and 4:4) we are told that God "added" large numbers of souls to the Church. The Greek word (*prostithemi*) means *"to add one thing to another."* It is a description of simple addition. By the time we reach Acts 4:4 (where the word "added" is not used, but the concept of addition is clear) God had added some 25,000 souls to the Church. That's not bad addition, and I certainly don't know of any pastor today who would turn

River Houses Rising

down 25,000 converts in less than a month's time (I sure wouldn't)!

But when we reach Acts 6:1 something changes. The word used to describe the growth of the Church changes from *prostithemi* ("addition") to a new word (*plethuno*) which is the Greek word meaning "to multiply." This new word appears in three more passages (Acts 6:7; 9:31 & 12:24) where the context clearly refers to multiplication. Here's the point: the growth of the early Church clearly moved from the SIMPLE ADDITION of people to the Church to the rapid MULTIPLICATION of people and Churches (the word for "add" is never used after Acts 6 to describe the growth of the early church)!

A Tale of Two Churches

Let's restate our point and then we will illustrate it. We will NEVER disciple the nations (the command of the Great Commission in Matthew 28:18-20) by means of simple addition (seeing how many converts we can add to our existing Church structures). Let's illustrate the problem by introducing you to two Churches: *The First Megachurch of Great Addition* and *The House Church of Simple Multiplication*.

Church #1: The First Megachurch of Great Addition. Each year of its existence *The First Megachurch of Great Addition* adds 25,000 new converts:

God Has A Math Problem

End of Year 1: 25,000 people
End of Year 2: 50,000 people
End of Year 3: 75,000 people
End of Year 4: 100,000 people
End of Year 5: 125,000 people
End of Year 6: 150,000 people
End of Year 7: 175,000 people
End of Year 8: 200,000 people
End of Year 9: 225,000 people
End of Year 10: 250,000 people
End of Year 11: 275,000 people

Church #2: The House Church of Simple Multiplication.
The House Church of Simple Multiplication ends its first year with 8 disciples, but each of those 8 disciples are committed to disciple eight more through their organic house church. *The House Church of Simple Multiplication* grows as follows:

End of Year 1: 8 people
End of Year 2: 64 people
End of Year 3: 512 people
End of Year 4: 4,096 people
End of Year 5: 32,768 people
End of Year 6: 262,144 people
End of Year 7: 2,097,152 people
End of Year 8: 16,777,216 people
End of Year 9: 134,217,728 people
End of Year 10: 1,073,741,824 people
End of Year 11: 8,589,934,592 people

River Houses Rising

O.K., Here is the quiz:

Question: In what year will *The House Church of Simple Multiplication* catch and pass *The First Megachurch of Great Addition*?

Answer: In Year 6. In other words, for the first five years the traditional *First Megachurch of Great Addition* will look wildly successful. In fact, they'll probably start their own Association of like-minded churches, and the Pastor and his staff will become wildly popular on the church growth speaker's circuit! Probably even write a book or two about how they did it and how you can do it, too! But somewhere during year six the novelty will be gone and reality will begin to set in. And that brings us to the two most critical questions.

Question: In what year will *The House Church of Simple Multiplication* fulfill the Great Commission?

Answer: Between years 10 and 11. Starting in year six *The House Church of Simple Multiplication* begins to demonstrate something phenomenal - a growth that borders on being exponential. And somewhere between years ten and eleven that growth reaches the population of the planet. But that is not so with *The First Megachurch of Great Addition*.

Question: In what year will *The First Megachurch of Great Addition* fulfill the Great Commission?

Answer: *NEVER!* Well, technically, it will take 274,963

God Has A Math Problem

years for it to reach the world's population by adding 25,000 per year, assuming that the world's population doesn't grow between now and then![36] Simply put, our current church structure combined with our current view of evangelism, resulting in a model of adding converts to existing boxes (or building new and bigger boxes to accommodate growth), **guarantees** our inability to accomplish the Church's primary calling - to disciple the nations. Then, when we consider that the sum total of all Christian workers and missionaries divided into the world's non-Christian population means that **each worker/missionary must disciple 9,335 people**, well, you get the picture (I hope!). Now, tell me, which sounds more feasible to you: discipling 9,335 people, or discipling 8 people in your organic house church. You do the math.

Questions For Reflection

Reflecting on this Chapter, how would you explain "God's Math Problem" in your own words to someone who had never heard of it before?

What is your personal strategy for raising up and equipping multiplying disciples through your organic house church?

Safe Houses of Hope And Prayer represent a strategy for discipling the nations through simple organic house church multiplication.

---

[36] The figure of 274,963 was arrived at by taking the world's current population of 6,874,078,491 and then dividing it by 25,000.

River Houses Rising

Chapter 14

Rabbits, Elephants And Mules

When it comes to the issues of organic growth, addition and multiplication it might be helpful if we begin with some basic biology. Specifically, let's talk about rabbits, elephants and mules.[37] We'll start with the mule. A mule is the offspring of a male donkey and a female horse. Because horses and donkeys are different species with different numbers of chromosomes (horses have 64 and donkeys have 62), their mule offspring are infertile. In short, mules are beasts of burden bred for extinction. They will never reproduce. Their DNA prevents it.

Rabbits, on the other hand, have no such problem. They reproduce like . . . well . . . like rabbits! The gestation cycle for a rabbit averages 31 days. Litter sizes generally range from 2-to-12 rabbits (called "kits"), and the new brood can reproduce by the time they are 3–to-4 months old. A mature female rabbit can be pregnant continuously for up to 9 months (called the "season"). An adult pair of healthy rabbits can produce up to 7 litters of offspring per season/year. One single pair of mature rabbits can easily produce 30-to-40 offspring per year. When the offspring of their offspring are

---

[37]My thanks to my friends Tony and Felicity Dale who have stimulated my thinking on this topic. See their book, ***The Rabbit and the Elephant: Why Small Is the New Big for Today's Church*** (Carol Stream, Illinois: Tyndale House Publishers, 2009).

River Houses Rising

included in the total, a pair of mature rabbits can produce 800 (yes, I said 800!) children, grand-children and great-grand-children in a single year. Talk about multiplication!

And then there's the elephant. The reproductive cycle of the elephant is long, slow and complex. Female elephants are not fertile until they are 12-to-14 years old (the same being roughly true of the male bull elephant, too). The gestation period for a pregnant elephant cow is twenty-two months. Generally speaking, mature elephant cows will produce one calf every 4-to-5 years, assuming conditions are favorable.

Which Are You?

There really is a point to this exercise in biology and reproduction. Figuratively speaking, all believers and churches fall into one of these three categories. All Christians are either mules, rabbits or elephants. Which are you? Which is your Church?

My experience is that most Christians and most Churches are "mules." Simply put, they never reproduce themselves. Indeed, like the mule, their very DNA prohibits it. Like the hard working mule, many of these "Christian mules" are active and even hard working in a wide variety of religious activities. Many of them are regarded as "pillars" or "backbones" of the Church, responsible for keeping the institution functioning in all of its many moving parts. But when it comes to the primary calling of the believer and the Church, namely, to make and multiply disciples, they are

Rabbits, Elephants And Mules

"spiritual mules." Both by model and by instruction, they have been given a DNA by the institution and its leadership that guarantees they will never reproduce. They have been bred for spiritual extinction. I would classify 80% of the existing Church as we know it as "spiritual mules."

If 80% of the existing Church as we know it is made up of spiritual mules which never reproduce, then I would classify about 15% of the existing Church as "spiritual elephants." These believers and these churches reproduce. But the process is slow and complex, requiring a large expenditure of effort and resources. Like the true elephants they are, reproducing themselves once every 5 years or so seems about normal.

A few "spiritual elephants" reproduce a bit more rapidly. A friend of mine is a missionary with the International Mission Board of the Southern Baptist Convention. In the particular country where he serves, the IMB came to a sobering realization. In the 40 years they had been active in that particular country they had planted 40 traditional Baptist Churches. In other words, they had given birth to one elephant per year for 40 years. For an elephant, that's rapid reproduction! But based upon this 40-year experience the IMB concluded that they would NEVER be able to reach that nation for Christ by planting more traditional churches ("spiritual elephants"). In other words, they realized that giving birth to more "spiritual elephants," even at the "unprecedented" rate of one per year, was not the answer to their dilemma. They made a conscious and intentional

River Houses Rising

decision to begin planting organic house churches. They decided to trade their herd of elephants in for a rabbit hutch. Since making that decision they have planted several hundred house churches, and the rabbits are starting to multiply!

Learning How To Multiply

O.K., if 80% of the existing Church is made up of "spiritual mules" and 15% is made up of "spiritual elephants," then that means that about 5% of the Church is made up of "spiritual rabbits" who multiply quickly. Now, the point of this whole "statistical exercise" is to ask a basic question: Why is it that some Churches multiply, while most DO NOT?!

Joel Comiskey is a well known leader in the Cell Church movement (the more organized cousin of the House Church movement). For his doctoral dissertation at Fuller Theological Seminary Joel studied 8 of the largest and fastest growing cell churches in the world and surveyed more than 700 cell group leaders. His goal was to discover why some cell leaders succeed while others fail at the task of evangelizing the lost and giving birth to new cell groups. His conclusions have subsequently been validated by other independent studies. [38]

As we think and pray about how to create a growing and

---

[38] Joel Comiskey, *Home Cell Group Explosion: How Your Small Group Can Grow And Multiply* (Houston: Touch Publications, 1998).

Rabbits, Elephants And Mules

multiplying house church, I believe that Joel's conclusions are as applicable to organic house churches as they are to cell churches. Here are two sets of Joel's conclusions. The first set of conclusions deals with those factors in the lives of leaders which DO NOT affect whether or not their churches multiply. The second set of conclusions deals with those factors in the lives of leaders which DO affect whether or not their churches multiply.

Factors That DO NOT Affect Multiplication

- The leader's gender, social class, age, marital (civil) status or education.

- The leader's personality type. Both introverted and extroverted leaders multiply their groups.

- The leader's spiritual gifting. Those with the gift of teaching, pastoring, mercy, leadership and evangelism equally multiply their groups.

Factors That DO Affect Multiplication

- The leader's devotional time. Those who spent 90 minutes or more in devotions per day multiplied their groups twice as much as those who spent less than 30 minutes! Time spent with God really is important!

- The leader's intercession for the participants.

River Houses Rising

Leaders who pray daily for the people in their groups are most likely to multiply their groups. Prayer really does make a difference. Who are you praying for?

- The leader spending time with God to prepare for a meeting. Spending time with God preparing the heart for a meeting is more important than preparing a lesson.

- Setting Goals. The leader who fails to set goals that the other participants know and remember has about a 50% chance of multiplying his or her group. Setting goals increases that chance to 75%.

- Knowing your multiplication date. Leaders who set specific goals - such as a date for giving birth and multiplying the group - consistently multiply their groups more often than leaders who do not set such goals. Remember the old adage: *"If you aim at nothing you'll hit it every time!"*

- Training. Leaders who feel better trained multiply their groups more rapidly. I prefer the word "equipping" over "training" because I believe that the biblical calling of gifted leadership (according to Ephesians 4:12) is to "equip" other leaders for the work of ministry.

- How often the leader contacts new people. Leaders

Rabbits, Elephants And Mules

who contacted five to seven new people per month had an 80% chance of multiplying their group.

My take away from this exercise is simply this: If we are going to experience a rapidly multiplying organic house church movement, it is going to require a greater degree of intentionality on our part. Are you ready to become intentional about seeing a multiplying organic house church in your house?

The Master's Plan of Multiplication

The above discussion was intended to help you gain some perspective on the practical factors (I'm calling these the "intentionality factors") which will most likely affect the multiplication of your organic house church, your *Safe House of Hope And Prayer*. People who ignore the practical aspects of reality are often disappointed with the outcome, so I would encourage you to take them seriously and become more intentional. I also want this discussion to challenge and encourage you to see that nothing prohibits YOU from leading an organic house church in your home and from seeing it grow and multiply.

But I also want to offer some additional perspective to help all of us better understand God's ultimate strategy behind discipleship, house church and multiplication. There is an older, somewhat neglected book about spiritual multiplication that I pull off the shelf and re-read every now and then entitled, ***The Master Plan of Evangelism*** by Robert

River Houses Rising

Coleman.[39] Whenever I read that book I am confronted with the reality that, for as long as I can remember (and I've been around long enough to remember a few things), the organized Church has done the opposite of what Jesus did. There has been a re-surge of interest in Dr. Coleman's book recently. But generally speaking Dr. Coleman's book is widely read but seldom followed. There is a reason for this. His book is an unintentional indictment of virtually everything the existing traditional organized Church does today. And we tend to avoid people who are that honest.

At the end of the day, most people with an IQ greater than that of a cucumber know when they are being used to further someone else's program. And most evangelism in the Church today (and for as long as I can remember) comes in the form of a program of some type (i.e., *"40 Days To A Purpose Driven Whatever,"* etc.). One of the problems with such programs is that they tend to use people as a means towards someone else's end. In addition, they have a fairly predictable life cycle. Once the cycle is over it is time for a new program and a new cycle starts all over again. If you haven't been through such a cycle more than once, then you haven't been involved in organized Church for very long.

But Jesus never used people to fulfill a program. He simply invested Himself in twelve key-but-unlikely people. Occasionally He would minister to the masses, but he poured

---

[39]Robert Coleman ***The Master Plan of Evangelism*** (Tarrytown, New York: Fleming H. Revell Company, 1972).

Rabbits, Elephants And Mules

Himself into twelve disciples, challenging their religion-shaped spirituality, slowly replacing it with one fashioned around Himself. Those twelve disciples *were* His plan, and the Kingdom of God was His program. Coleman describes it this way:

"Why did Jesus deliberately concentrate His life upon comparatively so few people? Had he not come to save the world? With the glowing announcement of John the Baptist ringing in the ears of multitudes, the Master easily could have had an immediate following of thousands if He wanted them. Why did He not then capitalize upon His opportunities to enlist a mighty army of believers to take the world by storm? Surely the Son of God could have adopted a more enticing program of mass recruitment. Is it not rather disappointing that one with all the powers of the universe at His command would live and die to save the world, yet in the end have only a few ragged disciples to show for His labors? The answer to this question focuses at once the real purpose of His plan for evangelism. Jesus was not trying to impress the crowd, but to usher in a Kingdom."[40]

From what I can tell from reading the New Testament, Jesus never concerned Himself with large numbers of converts. In fact, from what I have read in the Gospels, Jesus never concerned Himself with more than twelve (with the possible exception of training the 72 "others" in Luke 10). Why? *First,* because He knew how fickle the easily-led masses could be

---

[40]Coleman, ***The Master Plan of Evangelism***, p. 31.

River Houses Rising

(see John 2:23-25). Jesus understood that the same masses who would hail Him as King with loud Hosannas on Palm Sunday would trade Him for a murderer and cry out *"Crucify Him. We have no king but Caesar"* only one week later. That's fickle. *Second,* Jesus knew that the day would eventually come when the Holy Spirit, working through even one of those twelve Jesus-shaped, Kingdom-minded disciples, would sweep thousands into the Kingdom of God on a single day. But that day, He knew, would never come if He did not pour Himself into twelve illiterate fishermen, zealots, tax collectors and social outcasts, and if He did not prepare them to be clothed with power from on high. Succeed or fail, that was His plan. And it continues to be His plan today. The question we must ask ourselves is this: *"Is making 'disciples of the Kingdom' our plan, too?"*

It is ironic, but it really shouldn't surprise us, that whenever the Church has focused upon the masses we have eventually lost them. The history of the Church in America and its traditional love for crusades, mass meetings and megachurches should be sufficient proof of that. But we press ahead with more mass meetings and bigger churches in the firm but failed belief that "big is better," that next time we will *"do it right"* and that our latest big plan will succeed where others failed. When it comes to failed big programs, it seems that hope springs eternal in the heart of the unteachable. Coleman continues,

"Yet, strangely enough, it is scarcely comprehended in practice today. Most of the evangelistic efforts of the church

Rabbits, Elephants And Mules

begin with the multitudes under the assumption that the church is qualified to conserve what good is done. The result is our spectacular emphasis upon numbers of converts, candidates for baptism, and more members for the church, with little or no genuine concern manifested toward the establishment of these souls in the love and power of God, let alone the preservation and continuation of the work."[41]

The wisdom of Jesus' model of twelve has been demonstrated throughout church history during times of spiritual outpouring and revival. In the Evangelical Awakening of the mid-1700s John Wesley organized the entire Methodist Church into "Classes" of twelve people. The Methodist "Class" provided the engine of discipleship and growth for the Methodist Church for nearly 100 years.[42] Take note, because God is about to do it again.

George Barna argues that the traditional Church today is completely unprepared to handle the anticipated fruit of revival. According to Barna's research, a majority of the people who make a "decision" for Christ in one of our evangelical churches are not to be found in any church context within eight weeks of making that decision. This

---

[41] Coleman, ***The Master Plan of Evangelism***, p. 33.

[42] For an excellent treatment of the origins, functioning and demise of the Weslyan "Class of 12" structure, see David Francis Holsclaw, *"The Demise of Disciplined Christian Fellowship: The Methodist Class Meeting in Nineteenth-Century America,"* A Doctoral Dissertation in History in the Graduate Division of the University of California, Davis, 1982.

River Houses Rising

suggests that our current church infrastructure is not adequate to handle the results of normal activity, much less the overwhelming stress that comes upon the Church during times of revival, or from times of crisis and upheaval.

In response to this glaring need, I believe that God is raising up the tens of thousands of organic house churches, *Safe Houses of Hope And Prayer*, at this particular time in history in preparation to receive and to disciple the fruit of the coming revival. I believe that organic house church represents a return to the fundamental principle, modeled by Jesus Himself, of investing ourselves in a handful of people who, in their turn, will do the same with their own handful. It is the model Jesus taught and practiced, and it is the model He wants us to teach and practice, too.

So, how many people are in your organic house church, your *Safe House of Hope And Prayer*? If it's more than twelve, congratulations! You're doing better than Jesus ever did, so be encouraged. And what's your goal? Is your goal to impress the crowd, your traditional church friends or the faculty back at the denominational church planting office? Or is your goal to usher in a Kingdom? To impress the crowd will require big numbers. To usher in the Kingdom of God requires only twelve. Choose wisely which it will be. A simple organic house church of twelve committed disciples manifesting a Jesus-shaped spirituality could change the world. As Coleman observes:

"We should not expect a great number to begin with, nor

Rabbits, Elephants And Mules

would we desire it. The best work is always done with a few. Better to give a year or so to one or two men who learn what it means to conquer for Christ than to spend a lifetime with a congregation just keeping the program going. Nor does it matter how small or inauspicious the beginning may be; what counts is that those to whom we do give priority upon our life learn to give it away."[43]

It is time for us as "disciples of the Kingdom" to learn how to give it away, and to teach others to do the same.

Questions For Reflection

Reflecting on this Chapter, how would you characterize your most recent church experience: A rabbit? An Elephant? Or a Mule? Why?

What steps are you taking to insure that your organic house church experience will be different?

Safe Houses of Hope And Prayer represent a "spiritual rabbit hutch" living, growing and multiplying in your house. Elephants and mules need not apply.

---

[43] Coleman, ***The Master Plan of Evangelism***, p. 117.

River Houses Rising

Chapter 15

A Time To Network - Part 1

Small Flocks Unite!
By Paul H. Byerly [44]

I've been "doing" simple church for fifteen years now. I have been part of almost a dozen house churches, and have connections with many others. I have seen the good that comes from groups being connected. I have also seen the bad and ugly when groups go it alone.

The Good

My early simple church experience was with groups affiliated with Austin Fellowship – a far-flung network of simple church groups in the greater Austin, Texas area. I saw the power of a network many times.

A member of one group suffered a head injury leaving him unable to drive or work. He was the primary income for his family of seven, and they had limited savings. He had long-term disability at work, but it would not kick in for four

---

[44] This chapter is an excellent article by my friend, Paul Byerly. Paul and his wife Lori have been quiet leaders in the organic house church movement for many years. The article first appeared as an online article in House2House Magazine (http://house2housemagazine.com/) and is used here by permission.

River Houses Rising

months. It took only a couple of hours for the network to promise the family a substantial amount of money every month until his disability payments started. Many of those who gave to support this family had never met them, but they trusted those who told them the need was real.

When Mozambique was hit by massive flooding in the spring of 2000, Austin Fellowship did a great deal to help. Together we sent several doctors and nurses from our groups. These individuals offered medical help during the day and spiritual help in the evenings. They took thousands of dollars of medicine we were able to buy for pennies on the dollar due to the amount we purchased. Many lives were saved, both now and for eternity. Later the same year we collected clothing and shoes for orphans in Mozambique. Due to the large number of people involved, we collected, cleaned, sorted, and shipped a full sea container of quality items.

The Bad

Small groups lack the ability to help members who have significant problems. Financial issues are beyond the group, even if all give sacrificially. How many four or five family groups could financially support one of the families for months on end?

A lack of manpower and a shallow pool of skills limit how much help can be provided. A half-dozen strong backs is great, but it is not the same as 20 people showing up to help. Taking over the house and child care for a woman who is

Small Flocks Unite!

sick and unable to get out of bed is much easier with a larger network.

The Ugly

I have seen several groups destroyed because a single member or a family fell into some sin, or started to promote unbiblical doctrine. If these things are caught early enough solutions are possible, but all too often those who could help are too close to see the problem soon enough. Solo groups have no one they can ask for an outside opinion, and no uninvolved parties who can help moderate a difficult discussion. There is no loving help to get the group past its problems, and no place for individuals to go if the group folds.

All too often, the "trouble makers" in these situations go on to do the same to other groups. A lack of connection means there is no way to warn others. Wolves are free to roam from group to group, leaving a trail of carnage.

The Biblical

It is clear the early churches were connected. This was not a top down denominational structure, but a loose network. Those who were doing the work of the Lord were promoted across the network. Warnings were issued about those who caused problems. Groups helped and supported each other, and everyone benefitted.

River Houses Rising

If your simple church group is going it alone, you are in a dangerous and unbiblical situation. Look for a network, or find a few other groups and form a network. When your group grows and divides, stay in contact with each other. Know what is happening, what they need, and what they have to offer. Jesus called us to be part of His flock, not a lot of lone wolf groups!

Questions For Reflection

Reflecting on this article by Paul Byerly, what did you discover about organic house church networks that impressed you or stood out to you?

What stood out to you as perhaps the most important reason for being part of a house church network?

Chapter 16

A Time To Network - Part 2

Chicken For Lunch?

If you haven't seen the animated movie *"Chicken Run"* you should go rent a copy. It's a hoot! The chickens discover that they are destined to become chicken pot pies and hatch a plan to escape from the farm. Their vision: to become free range chickens. No farm. No attachments. No responsibilities. Live off the land. Do as they please.

Much of what I have personally witnessed in the house church movement over the years of my own personal involvement looks suspiciously like free range Christians. Having escaped the clutches of the institutional church they are intent upon becoming (or remaining) free range Christians. No institution. No organization. No responsibilities. No leadership. Live off the land. Just us and Jesus. Do as we please.

But I don't believe that is true elsewhere in the world. We are all somewhat awestruck by reports of house church networks around the world. I think of one such network in China with upwards of 10 million people in a single network. But notice something. The network, its participants and its leadership are both known and identifiable (otherwise, how would anyone know that there are ten million people in it?). There

River Houses Rising

is a recognizable degree of organization, accountability and leadership. There is also something else there in China that we here in America and the West don't have – PERSECUTION (although I believe this is about to dramatically change). When there is no external crisis or pressure, free range chickens, like free range Christians, can survive on their own (assuming of course that simple survival is the goal). But serious external pressure changes all that. Do you know what you call a free-range chicken under pressure? LUNCH!

Three Steps of Long-Term Success

Success in most areas of life requires a certain degree of intentionality. This reality is at the heart of the popular leadership maxim, *"Aim at nothing and you'll hit it every time."* Although house church is organic (growing in unanticipated ways), the pursuit of organic house church still requires a certain degree of intentionality on our part, as reflected in several basic questions, such as: When do you *intend* to start? Who do you *intend* to invite? What do you *intend* to do at your first gathering? Do you *intend* to study something in particular or leave that open for a while? And when do you *intend* to multiply by challenging others to repeat the process in their homes? And perhaps the most important question of all, *"Do you intend to raise up multiplying disciples of the Kingdom?"* In other words, do you *intend* to succeed on your journey into organic house church?

A Time To Network

If your answer to that last question was, *"Yes,"* then we need to spend a moment discussing what I call the *Three Steps of Long Term Success*. If your intended goal is to become the organic church which meets in your house, *A Safe House of Hope And Prayer*, and to become a vessel and new wineskin that God can use to disciple the nations in this upcoming spiritual outpouring, then I see three critical steps you should probably understand.

Step #1: Establish - This is probably where many, if not most, of you are right now. Some of you are thinking about starting a house church. My encouragement to you is very simple: *"Just Do It!"* Others of you have started but are still working on it. My encouragement to you is also simple: Ask for help. Good intentions are best expressed through good actions. Don't be a free range chicken. There is help and encouragement available if you'll just ask for it. The goal of this book and of the *Safe Houses of Hope And Prayer* network is to encourage you to believe that God is at work and He wants to establish you. And we want to help you get established, too.

Step #2: Multiply - Some of you have already completed *Step #1*. In fact, you completed it a long time ago and have been "established" for quite some time. And that's the problem. You haven't reproduced at all. And you certainly haven't multiplied. You have become a "spiritual mule" (see the previous chapter). I have received e-mails from house churches saying, *"We don't know what to do. Our leadership doesn't have any vision beyond just meeting together."* The

River Houses Rising

ultimate test of effectiveness and viability for any organic house church is the number of times it has reproduced itself (multiplied). If there has been no reproduction or multiplication, everyone involved must seriously ask the question, *"Why?"* What's your intention when it comes to reproducing (yep, we're back to the whole intentionality thing, again!)? What's wrong with your spiritual DNA? Why are you not contagious and growing? And what needs to change?

Step #3: Network - To understand this third step we should review a verse from the Book of Acts,

"And day by day continuing with one mind in the temple, and breaking bread from house to house, they were taking their meals together with gladness and sincerity of heart" (Acts 2:46, NASB).

Did you notice the part about meeting "house to house"? When we read in the book of Acts that the early church met from house to house it should become immediately apparent that these early house churches were inter-connected. This becomes unavoidably apparent when we consider that by the end of Acts Chapter 4 somewhere in around 25 thousand people had been added to the Church in Jerusalem.[45] Where

---

[45] Acts 2:41 says three thousand people were added to the church that day, while Acts 4:4 adds another five thousand (for a total of eight thousand), and these numbers only counted men as "heads of households." Assuming that each household consisted of at least 4 people (husband, wife and two kids -probably a low figure), this would yield a total number closer to 32,000 people added to the Church. I have "deflated" that

A Time To Network

did they meet? If the average house church in Jerusalem contained 25 people (four or five families meeting together), that would suggest a house church network of 1,000 house churches in Jerusalem! It is reasonable to assume that they were networked together, in order to be able to meet in one another's homes ("house to house"). And the leaders of the various house churches must have known and interacted with one another. They also would have known and interacted with the 5-fold leadership (apostles, prophets, evangelists, pastors and teachers) in Jerusalem as they traveled among and ministered in the various house churches. For example, the church in Jerusalem had apostles and elders who met with the apostles and elders of other churches to solve problems (See Acts Chapter 15).

This kind of inter-connectedness and networking requires at least two things. **First**, it requires intentionality on your part to network with other like-minded disciples in pursuit of organic house church and life in the Kingdom of God. **Second**, it requires building relationships of trust within the wider body of Christ. Are you ready to network?

The Importance of Networking. Why are networks of house churches going to be so important in the days ahead? *First*, because networks of house churches will be the channel and vessel for the next great movement of the Spirit of God in renewal and revival. *Second*, because networks of house churches will provide a persecution resistant structure to

---

number down to 25,000, just to be "fair."

River Houses Rising

protect and encourage God's people through the difficult times that may lie ahead (See Chapter 4, *"Red Skies And House Churches"*).

Let's be blunt. Let me be somewhat blunt and to the point for just a moment. I do not believe that either you or your house church will survive, grow or multiply long-term if you are not networked with other like minded believers and house churches who can offer you support, encouragement, equipping, teaching, counseling and more.

That's not our role. It is our role or place (or anyone's role or place, for that matter) to tell you how to manage and lead your organic house church. Our calling and our mission is to encourage you to become the church that meets in your house and to provide you with the equipping and resources that you need to succeed. That is the most that ANY organization or network can do.

We look forward to networking with you!

Is Your Boat On Fire?

In 1518 a thirty-three year old conquistador landed in Mexico with 11 ships, 500 men, 13 horses and a small number of cannons. He was shocked to find the Aztecs taking prisoners of the weaker tribes, ripping their hearts out atop temples, and, in a frenzy, eating their bodies. The conquistador freed the prisoners, knocked down idols, and erected crosses. His name was Hernando Cortez. His personal secretary,

A Time To Network

Francisco Lopez de Gomara, wrote: *"Cortez told them of their blindness . . . in worshiping many gods and making sacrifices of human blood . . . He then told them of a single God, Creator of Heaven and earth . . . whom all men should worship and serve."*

When Cortez landed in the New World he knew that the greatest danger facing his troops was not the natives but his men's own fears. And the greatest temptation they faced was the temptation to yield to their fears, re-board their ships and return to Spain. So Cortez ordered his men to strip the ships of everything useable . . . and then to set them on fire. Cortez burned his ships so that he and his men would have no choice but to survive and to conquer. Regardless of whatever other faults he may have had (and he had many), Hernando Cortez understood the cost of victory. Do we?

At this point I can't help but ask a question: What is your "Kingdom vision" for what you want to see God do in your life? And what price are you willing to pay to see God fulfill that vision? In my own life and ministry I have discovered that Kingdom visions come with spiritual price tags attached. And on those tags I find the prices spelled out in words, like: pride, lifestyle, reputation, material comfort, traditions. And the fine print on the price tag declares, *"This kingdom vision will cost you all of these things."*

To put it another way, *"What is it you want God to do in your life, in the life of your family, and in your ministry, and what price are you willing to pay to see Him do that?"* Answer that

River Houses Rising

question and I can tell you what God is about to do in your life and ministry.

Safe Houses of Hope And Prayer represents the tangible expression our Kingdom vision is to see God give birth to a genuine movement of His Spirit which flows through tens of thousands of organic house churches led by Kingdom-minded believers in pursuit of a Jesus-Shaped spirituality just like you. I believe it will be in these organic house churches, like the one meeting in your house, that our generation will experience God's Kingdom Presence and His Kingdom Power as He turns our homes into places of power, peace and healing. This is our vision. And this is your invitation to join us!

The story of *Safe Houses of Hope And Prayer* continues in our next book, **Safe Houses Of Hope And Prayer: Your Practical Guide To Organic Church In Your House**, available on our website from Amazon.com.

www.risingrivermedia.org

www.ingramcontent.com/pod-product-compliance
Lightning Source LLC
Chambersburg PA
CBHW060539100426
42743CB00009B/1572